SCOTLAND IN TRUST

Her Majesty Queen Elizabeth The Queen Mother
and The Earl of Wemyss and March at Falkland
Palace in 1981.

Jenni Calder

SCOTLAND IN TRUST

The National Trust for Scotland

Published in association with

🛡 National Trust for Scotland

THE PRESERVATION PRESS
NATIONAL TRUST FOR HISTORIC PRESERVATION

The Preservation Press
National Trust for Historic Preservation
1785 Massachusetts Avenue, N.W.
Washington, D.C. 20036

The National Trust for Historic Preservation in the
United States is the only private nonprofit
organization chartered by Congress to encourage
public participation in the preservation of sites,
buildings and objects significant in American
history and culture. Support is provided by
membership dues, endowment funds, contributions and
grants from federal agencies, including the U.S.
Department of the Interior, under provisions of
the National Historic Preservation Act of 1966.
The opinions expressed in this publication do not
necessarily reflect the views or policies of the
Interior Department. For information about
membership, write to the Trust at the above address.

Library of Congress Cataloging in Publication Data

Calder, Jenni.
    Scotland in trust / Jenni Calder.
        p.   cm.
    ISBN 0-89133-162-X
    1. National Trust for Scotland—History. 2. Historic buildings—
Scotland—Conservation and restoration. 3. Historic sites—
Scotland—Conservation and restoration. 4. Architecture—Scotland—
Conservation and restoration. 5. Nature conservation—Scotland.
6. Scotland—Antiquities.   I. Title.
DA873.C35   1990
941.1—dc20   90—43558

Orginally published in Scotland by
Richard Drew Publishing Limited

Printed and bound in Great Britain
98 97 96 95 94 93 92 91   5 4 3 2 1

Designed by James W. Murray
Color reproduction by Arneg Limited, Glasgow
Phototypeset by David J. Clark, Glasgow
Printed and bound by
Butler & Tanner Limited, Frome and London

Contents

Acknowledgements

I am very grateful to Lester Borley, Director of the National Trust for Scotland, Charles Tyrrell, Chairman of Council and Executive Committee, Sir Jamie Stormonth Darling, and all those at the National Trust for Scotland who have assisted this project in many different ways. I would also like to thank Hugh Cheape for his help with information, and Bruce Lenman and Iseabail Macleod for their invaluable comments on the first draft.

All photographs in this book, with the exception of page 48, The raising of the standard (National Galleries of Scotland) and page 111, Culzean Castle (James W Murray), are from the Photo Library at the National Trust for Scotland.

Foreword
BY THE EARL OF WEMYSS AND MARCH

Over the sixty years that the National Trust for Scotland has been in existence, many books have been written about it in general and its properties in particular. With the Diamond Jubilee of the Trust falling next year, it is particularly appropriate that Jenni Calder has written such a carefully researched book taking a long view of the Trust and its many and varied activities.

In 1932, just a year after the creation of the National Trust for Scotland, Sir John Stirling Maxwell, one of its founders, wrote: 'the Trust serves the nation as a cabinet into which it can put some of its valuable things, where they will be perfectly safe for all time and where they will be open to be seen and enjoyed by everyone'. Jenni Calder has dipped deep into this 'cabinet' which has increased in size one hundredfold since Sir John wrote those prophetic words.

In the book, she has painted a wonderful word picture showing how the chequered history of Scotland is inter-twined with the families associated with so many of the Trust's properties. And, within these covers, the reader will also learn a lot about Scotland and its social and political history. Much too is revealed about how the infant Trust, with little funds but lots of enthusiasm, progressed and developed over the past 60 years to become the important, creditable organization and champion of conservation that it is today.

'Ive seen sae mony changefu' years' wrote Robert Burns. With regard to the National Trust for Scotland, I share the Bard's sentiments having been a Life Member for over 50 years and associated with the Council of the Trust for all but five of those years. This book welds together the 'changefu' years' and reveals the real contribution made to Scotland by its very own National Trust.

CHAPTER ONE

The Land

SCOTLAND has been the scene of human activity for around nine thousand years. During these millennia the configuration of the land and the influence of the climate have given distinctive shape to Scottish lives. It is a distinctiveness of community and of the individual, which cannot be separated from its environment, and which is the result of the most intimate relationship between nature and humanity. It is this relationship that is at the heart of Scottish history.

All nations, of course, are the product to some extent of their physical environment: Scotland is extraordinarily so. It is indelibly stamped, in character and history, by its geological foundation and its ecological structure. This is where an understanding of Scotland begins, and it is where the National Trust for Scotland begins. The Trust's foundation in 1931 owed much to a growing concern with the erosion of both the natural and the built environment. This concern had already brought into existence the National Trust in England and the Association for the Preservation of Rural Scotland. The creation of a separate National Trust for Scotland, with the power to hold and manage property, was a further step not just in the registering of concern but in the implementation of needful action.

From the beginning the National Trust for Scotland was as attentive to the landscape itself as to the evidence of Scotland's human history. Indeed, the landscape *is* evidence of Scotland's human history, for everywhere reveals the consequences of the human struggle for survival. Once-forested hillsides are bare, the results of thousands of years of tree felling. Only fragments of the original Caledonian forest survive. Towns and cities obscure the landscape, but remote ruins and moorland paths are equally the outward signs of the lives of men and women.

The face of the landscape that we think of as characteristically Scottish, the mountains and lochs, the glens and straths, the rugged coastline, has been moulded partly by the constant labour to provide food and shelter. The wildlife that this landscape sustains has been affected by the same labour. And this endeavour, and the activities consequent upon it, are the main highway of Scotland's past, linking the lives of pre-history with our own today.

Most people, visitor and native alike, if asked to indicate the most notable feature of the Scottish countryside, probably mention mountains. But mountains are only one of the many striking attributes of a very diverse landscape. The richly fertile Lothians, the Southern Uplands which separate them from England, the broad firths and deep

Fingal's Cave, Island of Staffa.

sea lochs, the islands from the Bass Rock to St Kilda, the green straths and the dark moors, all make their distinctive contribution. They have all shaped Scotland's past and Scotland's present. Equally, Scottish history has been shaped by a division between Highland and Lowland. Every invader of Scotland was affected by it; every attempt to rule Scotland encountered it.

In the eighteenth century the division received particular emphasis. This came partly as a result of the Union of 1707, which shifted the centre of government from Edinburgh to London. The Jacobite Risings contributed, and so did the intellectual and cultural explosion that is known as the Scottish Enlightenment. New ideas and innovations in practice affected philosophy and agriculture, science and manufacture, art and literature — in other words, underlined the difference between the civilized and the cultivated, and the wild and untamed. Industrialization continued this emphasis, and by tempting people away from the unproductive Highlands made those parts of Scotland seem both less accessible and less acceptable.

Industrialization had the effect of divorcing people from the land and disrupting that close relationship. By the early nineteenth century the Highlands were seen by some as a rural slum, and travellers in the previous centuries had often been as much struck by the country's barbarity as by its scenic splendour. But parallel to the growing depopulation of the Highlands, a combination of the pull of the cities, with their promise of employment, and the push of landowners who saw that the hills could sustain sheep more economically than men, was the growing appeal of the picturesque. A romantic response to mountains and rivers was much encouraged by the poems and novels of Sir Walter Scott, whose work was read throughout Europe and contributed to bringing the Highlands of Scotland back into the mainstream of European consciousness. Later in the century Queen Victoria's love of Scotland fostered this interest in the Highlands. Wild landscapes became fashionable. Revolutions in transport and the changing circumstances of travel brought visitors to Scotland, and particularly north of the Highland Line, who not so many decades before would have regarded the journey as a risky adventure.

At the same time as this growth in romantic interest came a sharpening of scientific awareness. By the 1840s Scotland had become a focus of international geological interest. The age and variety of the rocks provided vital evidence about the structure of the landscape. There is also the fossil evidence, some of it the testimony of life four hundred million years ago. Amongst the many geologists who collected and described Scotland's fossils was Hugh Miller, whose books on geology, especially *The Old Red Sandstone* (1841), were bestsellers and did more than anything else to establish the popularity of this very new science. The cottage at Cromarty in which Hugh Miller grew up is now in the Trust's care.

THE LAND

There was an equal interest in living evidence. The botanist and the zoologist, professional and amateur, male and female, were also attracted to the wild, and sometimes not so wild, areas. Professor Robert Jameson of Edinburgh University led his students out on field excursions and inspired many future naturalists and geologists. Others, like John Muir, born in Dunbar in 1838, were self-taught: Muir, a promoter of the National Parks idea in America, has been described as 'the father of conservation'.

These currents of romantic and scientific response often merged. They both contributed to an awareness of the crucial value of the natural environment. The understanding of the intimate relationship between the survival of the natural world and human wellbeing may not have been so urgent as it is now, but, as the writings of John Muir reveal, there was a significant appreciation of the landscape and its life. The proliferation of industrial blight and urban sprawl only emphasized this consciousness.

Thus, the conservation movement had its origins in the nineteenth century, and the stimulus of Scotland's landscape to the mind and the imagination had helped to nurse it through infancy. The National Trust for Scotland was founded in 1931, and its approach and aspirations were influenced by the National Trust, by that time in existence for thirty-six years, and by the National Parks movement in the United States. Both the Trust in Scotland and its older sister have a commitment to the preservation of 'Places of Historic Interest or Natural Beauty', and in Scotland the emphasis on the countryside is particularly strong. One of the first properties to be acquired by the National Trust for Scotland was Burg, Isle of Mull, bequeathed to the Trust in 1932 by Mr A Campbell Blair of Dolgelly. Its character and remoteness sum up an essential aspect of the Trust. It represents not conventional scenic beauty, but something rather more harsh and more demanding.

Across the water is Burg, Isle of Mull, the first countryside property to come to the Trust.

Burg is situated on the western tip of the Ardmeanach peninsula. Vehicles can reach a point five miles distant from Burg Farm on a Forestry Commission road, with a rough track continuing thereafter. This difficulty of access has meant an inevitable decline of human habitation. In the 1930s, a time of serious depression in the Highlands, the Trust was instrumental in making active efforts to revive farming. Burg Farm was in a nearly derelict state, with many acres of pasture taken over by bracken, the stock in poor condition, and poor yields from the crops. With grants from the Pilgrim Trust, an organization that played a vital part in the Trust's early years, and advice from Dr David Russell and the West of Scotland College of Agriculture, efforts were made to eradicate the bracken, revive the arable land and improve the stock. There were improvements, too, to the farmhouse and steading, and a new pier was built: communications were rightly seen as the key to success. But these efforts to reclaim the land and revitalize the farm proved unsuccessful, although the first historian of the Trust, Robert Hurd, writing in 1939, was full of hope.

For many years the late Chrissie McGillivray of Burg Farm, whose family had farmed there for several generations, presided over fifteen hundred acres of wilderness, a haven for wildlife if not for humanity. It is also of considerable interest to the geologist. In addition to basalt columns similar to the more famous examples of Staffa, also in the Trust's care, there is the fossilized imprint of a tree, known as MacCulloch's Tree, about fifty million years old, which can be reached at low tide. Today the visitor who walks that last five miles to Burg will find a landscape that has resisted attempts to tame it. It is now richly populated by red deer, wild goat, otters and many species of birds, including golden plover.

Another untamed area that came early to the Trust is Glencoe, but here a main artery of Scotland's road network brings hundreds of thousands of visitors. Glencoe's formidable mountains are within reach of everyone with wheels. In 1935 the Glencoe estate of Lord Strathcona came on the market. The Trust was interested, and decided to bid for the lot that included Torren and the Signal Rock. Accordingly, Arthur Russell, the Trust's law agent, accompanied by his son George (who later held the same post), went to Glencoe for the auction. The night before they camped near the Clachaig Hotel. In the hotel that evening the Russells got into conversation with a Dr Sutherland who was also interested in Torren. After some discussion Dr Sutherland made a generous offer: if he secured Torren he would donate the Signal Rock to the Trust. He was successful, which meant that the Trust acquired the Signal Rock, and had money with which to purchase another part of the estate. Later, Arthur Russell was able to negotiate the purchase of the glen itself, including the famous Aonach Eagach ridge, with the help of Lord Strathcona and members of the Scottish Mountaineering Club.

Thus were the first steps in Glencoe accomplished. The next step

The ridge of Aonach Eagach, Glencoe.

came a little over a year later, when the Scottish Mountaineering Club proposed purchasing the estate of Dalness, adjoining the area already acquired, and presenting it to the Trust. The Club raised the money, £6,500, through a national appeal, although the bulk of it was actually donated anonymously by the Club's president, Percy Unna. The Pilgrim Trust also contributed, and much of that donation went into an endowment fund. Within two years, with twenty square miles of Glencoe in its care, the Trust had expanded its countryside responsibilities immensely.

In addition to Aonach Eagach the Trust had now acquired a cluster of some of Scotland's most impressive peaks. The highest were Bidean nam Bian (1150 metres) on the south side of Glencoe and Buachaille Etive Mor (1020 metres), which looks down over both Glencoe and Glen Etive to the south-east. Aonach Dubh features spectacular rock faces, while the narrow ridge of Aonach Eagach must be one of the most dramatic in Scotland. There is a quality of ominous isolation in Glencoe, which owes as much to the landscape itself as to its historical associations. It is dangerous country, wild and sparsely populated. When Charles Dickens visited the glen in 1841 he remarked 'anything so bleak and wild and mighty in its loneliness . . . it is impossible to conceive. Glencoe itself is perfectly *terrible*. The pass is an awful place . . . there are scores of glens, high up, which form such haunts as you might imagine yourself wandering in, in the very height and madness of

Percy Unna through whose initiatives and support the Trust acquired parts of Glencoe and Torridon and other mountain properties.

a fever.' And H V Morton, who quotes this passage from Dickens in his book *In Search of Scotland* (1929), adds that the glen with its mountains is 'a lesson in humility'.

The area's harsh aspect is the result of its geological origins, ancient schists more than 500 million years old, overlaid by volcanic activity, and scoured by glaciers and erosion. The dark exposed rock is a prominent feature. At first sight Glencoe seems barren. Most of the trees have gone, but there is a wealth of moorland and mountain flora, including, on the higher slopes, a number of alpine species. The lack of trees means there is little shelter for wildlife, but resident in Glencoe are the blue hare, the pine marten, the red squirrel and the wildcat, as well as more familiar species. There is a flourishing and diverse bird population which includes amongst the rarer species the snow bunting, the ptarmigan and, least common of all, the dotterel.

When Percy Unna, with his mountaineering associates, lent his support to the Trust, taking the initiative on Dalness and raising money, he expressed strong views on the need to protect and preserve the wilderness. By the 1930s Glencoe had had its share of famous visitors, including Wordsworth and Queen Victoria as well as Dickens, and was familiar territory to walkers and climbers, but it was not the tourist attraction that it has since become. Unna was committed to keeping the wilderness wild. At the same time he believed that access to the public should be unrestricted. But he did not wish access to be made easier, for either the driver or the walker. He disapproved of signposts and cairns, and anything of the kind which intruded on the landscape. Although he foresaw a heightened awareness of the pleasures of the countryside he could scarcely have envisaged the numbers that tour, stroll, picnic, walk and climb in Glencoe today.

The attraction is not only the wildness. Glencoe is immersed in legend and history. As well as tales of witches and monsters there are associations with Fingal who, according to legend, defeated the Vikings (although he must have lived well before the Viking invasions) in a series of set battles near Ballachulish, and with Ossian. Place-names reflect this: there is Fionn Ghleann (Fingal's glen), and Ossian's cave, high up on Aonach Dubh. The legendary Deirdre lived in nearby Glen Etive. She sang her famous lament as the galley taking her to Ireland with Fergus, Knight of the Red Branch, sailed down Loch Etive. In historic times Glencoe, which probably never had more than 500 inhabitants, is linked with many significant phases in Scottish history, from the coming of Christianity to the Jacobite rising of 1745. The Massacre of 1692, which overshadows all other episodes, was only one of many bloody encounters that involved the people of the glen. The countryside itself is redolent of some of the darker and more symbolic aspects of Scotland's history.

From the start the area posed a challenge to the conservation remit of the Trust. The problem, replicated in scenic and historic areas all over

Scotland, was to encourage understanding of the environment and its history without damaging the features that made it so valuable. Inevitably, the numbers of visitors steadily increased. On the one hand it was necessary to fend off excessive and inappropriate tourist development; on the other it was important to provide for the tourists who came in growing numbers.

At a conference in 1959 on 'Tourism and the Countryside', which followed the Trust's Annual General Meeting of that year, it was suggested that there were serious deficiencies in the general provision of basic facilities for the visitor. The lack of good roads and stopping places, of litter collection and toilet facilities, was detrimental both to the visitor and to the countryside. Yet it was vital that such provision should not get out of proportion. In 1962 there was a proposal to build a motel and petrol station at Altnafeadh, between the Etive crossroads and the entrance to the Pass of Glencoe. The Trust lodged a formal objection, and there followed a public inquiry in September of that year. Planning permission was refused. A statement made the criteria for future development clear.

> *On general policy grounds, the Secretary of State considers that the vital core of areas of landscape value of the type of Glencoe, which depend for their effect on starkness and the almost complete absence of the appearance of human settlement, should be kept inviolate, and that necessary tourist development should be restricted to subsidiary adjoining areas.*

Glencoe Visitor Centre.

In the 1960s there was a growing awareness of the need both of protecting the environment and providing for the tourist. Indeed, in some of the remoter parts of Scotland the economy depended on the encouragement of tourism. The challenge was to ensure that development was controlled and responsible. Attentiveness to these problems was reflected in the Duke of Edinburgh's study conferences on 'The Countryside in 1970'. Out of these was born a working group on 'Countryside: Planning and Development in Scotland', whose recommendations led to the Countryside (Scotland) Act of 1967 which established the Countryside Commission for Scotland with responsibilities for both conservation and improving facilities. The Commission has been an effective partner with the Trust on a number of projects.

As a result of the Trust's 1959 conference steps were taken to provide more facilities in Glencoe. In July 1962 Lord Cameron opened a visitor centre provided for the Trust by Scottish Oils and Shell-Mex Ltd, and inaugurated a litter collection scheme. Fourteen years later something more substantial was needed, and a new visitor centre, built by the Countryside Commission for Scotland and run by the Trust, was opened at Clachaig. This provides information on the history of the glen and on mountaineering. A mile or so away are the Mountain Rescue

Post and the Leishman Memorial Centre, which conducts research into mountain safety.

One of the most significant developments in the conservation and interpretation of the countryside has been the ranger service initiated by the Trust in 1969 with the financial assistance of the Countryside Commission for Scotland. The following year generous grants from the MacRobert Trusts enabled the setting up of training courses for rangers, which continued until the Countryside Commission for Scotland took over the training of rangers in 1974. The rangers provide a vital link between the environment and the visitor. They are naturalists, with considerable knowledge and experience of the area in which they work, and they are communicators. They combine countryside management with an educational role, maintaining and protecting the environment while providing guidance to visitors and leading groups on walks and projects. Recently biological surveys of the Trust's properties (including designed landscapes as well as the wilder countryside) have been initiated, and these also involve the rangers.

In the 1940s a number of Perthshire properties came to the Trust, which represent some of the very varied terrain of the area. Although they include nothing quite as magnificently daunting as Glencoe they embrace the wilder as well as the gentler aspects of the Perthshire landscape. For many Perthshire is an introduction to the Highlands. As the A9 speeds travellers north the more benign Lowlands seem to merge easily into the rugged hills and glens that unfold on either side. The historical resonances are as varied as the landscape. Powerful families have had their base in Perthshire. Troops have crisscrossed the hills and battles have been fought. Trade and towns have flourished; landowners have improved and planted.

From the top of Craigower Hill, near Pitlochry, given to the Trust in 1947 by Mrs M D Fergusson of Baledmund in memory of her father, Captain G A K Wisely, the view spreads out to the south, west and north. Craigower is a kind of meeting point. The fertile Tay Valley stretches south, having taken its great bend from the west. The Tay itself, and its tributaries, are crucial to an understanding of Perthshire. On its banks are the towns that were the focal point of so much of the area's activity, trade and trysts, small-scale industry, gatherings peaceful and warlike. Looking west from Craigower there are Loch Tummel and beyond that the desolate moor of Rannoch leading to Glencoe, and a turn to the north brings to view the Pass of Killiecrankie. Further to the north are the more massive heights of Beinn Dearg and Beinn a' Chait.

Craigower Hill is an excellent spot from which to take in a generous helping of the Highlands. Within the panorama is the Linn of Tummel, which came to the Trust in 1944 as a gift from Dr G F Barbour of Bonskeid. The Linn (Gaelic *linne* meaning 'pool') marks the meeting point of the rivers Garry and Tummel. At one time the Tummel joined the Garry in an impressive waterfall, but when the Loch Faskally reservoir was created the water levels changed and the falls diminished. However, there still survives a fish pass, a forty-foot long tunnel, which enabled salmon to avoid the falls.

1970, European Conservation Year, saw the creation of a forest nature trail which takes the walker along the banks of both rivers. It is a richly wooded area, with both native and imported trees, the latter including the Douglas fir brought from North America by David Douglas in 1827. Douglas was born at Scone, and the original fir still stands in the grounds of Scone Palace.

Up the Garry from the Linn of Tummel the river has carved a deep and narrow channel, the Pass of Killiecrankie. In 1947 Mrs Edith Foster gifted the area to the Trust. The exit from the Pass to Blair Castle and the north saw the clash between 'Bonnie Dundee' and government troops in 1689. But it is also an area that is environmentally distinctive and characteristic. The narrow gorge resulted from the strength of the rock, mica-schist with bands of stronger quartzite, which resisted the pressure of the Ice Age glaciers. The woodland is similar to that of the Linn of Tummel, with native Scots pine, oak and birch, and the aspen which inspired the name of the Pass — *coille creithnich*, 'the shaking wood'. But there are several imported species, of which beech in particular is a problem. Beech spreads easily and rapidly. The mature trees cast a heavy shade, threatening native species which are adapted to regenerate in less shady conditions. The result is that the invading beech is in danger of taking over.

Efforts are now being made to protect the native species. Beech are being cut down to admit more light, and there has been some replanting. The native seedlings are protected by tree guards. This kind of management is necessary to regain a balance, a balance that was disrupted in the first place by human activity. It assists not only the regeneration of native trees, but survival of shrubs and small plant life that flourished in the native woodlands.

The need to protect vegetation is particularly evident at another of the Trust's Perthshire properties. South and west of Killiecrankie rises the Tayside mountain of Ben Lawers, 1214 metres high, and an unrivalled Scottish habitat for alpine flora. It has been described as 'the largest and finest rock garden in the country'. The extent of the botanical richness of Ben Lawers was first discovered in the late eighteenth century, and since then it has attracted great interest. The special nature of this habitat is the result of a combination of geology and climate. The mountain is the result of the folding of sedimentary rocks, activity which took place about 500 million years ago. The original limey shales of these rocks have left a high lime content in the soil. This, with the fact that Ben Lawers rocks have broken up into schists, thin layers, which in turn become mineral-rich soil, has encouraged a vigorous plant life, particularly high up on the mountain.

Ben Lawers, a unique habitat for alpine flora.

Footpath maintenance is a major concern on countryside properties. At work on a path in Glen Rosa, Arran (above left) and the result (above right). A path on Ben Lawers before (below left) and after (below right) maintenance.

In the summer the saxifrages, gentians, alpine mouse-ear, moss campion and mossy cyphel especially attract attention. But as with most environments, Ben Lawers has its conservation problems. The area is heavily grazed by sheep, and the practice of burning heather has been a threat to many species. The tough survivor of this pressure is *Nardus* grass, which sheep avoid, and which grows so densely that other species are excluded. Ben Lawers is a striking example of the need to get the balance right between human, animal and plant requirements. Efforts are being made to protect small areas of plant life by putting up exclosure fences to keep out sheep and deer. Many areas in the Highlands face the same problem. On Ben Lawers the intensity of the sheep-grazing is itself a reflection of the rich vegetation originally available. Some of the rarer species have survived only on ledges too narrow for grazing.

The mountain was acquired by the Trust in 1950, again through the generosity of Percy Unna. From 1963 the Nature Conservancy Council worked with the Trust to establish an information centre, which was opened in 1966, and in 1967 a seasonal warden began work. Later, grants from the Countryside Commission for Scotland, the Carnegie UK Trust and Perthshire County Council contributed to the extension of services for the visitor. Since 1972 there has been a full-time ranger-naturalist managing the site and providing information for the public, information which has both an educational and protective purpose. Since 1975 Ben Lawers has been a National Nature Reserve, managed jointly by the Trust and the Nature Conservancy Council. As with all the Trust's countryside properties policy has focused on habitat management rather than the protection of single species.

Ben Lomond.

Management of the countryside is not a new activity in the area. In 1600 Sir Duncan Campbell of Glenorchy encouraged his tenants to plant trees, and provided saplings of oak, ash and plane at two pennies each. The 'wanton destruction' of trees was heavily fined. But inevitably the changes in farming practice which came with the eighteenth century permanently affected the landscape. The old runrig system of raising crops gave way to enclosure. The potato was introduced and replaced flax, which supplied the Perthshire linen industry, as a major crop. A new understanding of the value of crop rotation and the use of manures brought improved yields, but the next century saw a reduction of arable land and the growing presence on the slopes of sheep, with the consequent effects on vegetation.

The control of sheep and deer is a leading consideration of the Trust's countryside management policy. At Ben Lomond, purchased by the Trust in 1984 with a grant from the Countryside Commission for Scotland and anonymous benefactors, conservation is being developed with the resources of an endowment contributed to by the National Heritage Memorial Fund. The current emphasis is on combining the needs of agriculture and the preservation of the environment. A good working relationship with local farmers has enabled the building of wintering sheds for sheep, thus reducing grazing on Ben Lomond. Exclosure fences are keeping out the deer. These measures encourage the regeneration of heather and shrubs, as well as of the oak woodland.

In the north-west of Scotland the Trust cares for some of the most impressive and fascinating mountain landscape in the country. Torridon came to the Trust in 1967, after the death of the fourth Earl of Lovelace. His 14,000 acre estate was accepted by the Inland Revenue in lieu of death duties. It includes three great mountains, Liathach (1054 metres), Beinn Eighe (972 metres) and Beinn Alligin (985 metres), all a temptation to the mountaineer and natural historian alike. For the geologist in particular Torridon is a focus of interest. The Torridonian

Beinn Alligin (centre), Torridon.

Lea MacNally, ranger at Torridon, with a red deer calf.

sandstones, 750 million year old, are the oldest in Scotland. The mountains have an unrivalled dramatic grandeur, highlighted by the glittering quartzite which embellishes Liathach and Beinn Eighe. Fossils of some of the earliest animals on earth have been found in the Beinn Eighe rock. The particular significance of the Torridonian sandstones lies in the fact that for millions of years they have remained relatively unaltered. Earth movements and glaciation have tilted, gouged and smoothed the rock, and the weather has left its marks, but the nature of the rock itself has changed little.

There are live animals to be found as well as fossils, red deer and roe deer, fox and wild goat, seal, otter and pine marten. Amongst the birds golden eagle, peregrine, kestrel, merlin and sparrowhawk, tawny owl, greenshank, grouse and ptarmigan and black- and red-throated diver are notable. The vegetation includes mountain azalea and a number of alpine species. Here, too, in spite of the fact that Torridon is wilder and more remote than Perthshire, conservation is a challenge. The red deer is a major problem facing both the Trust and the Nature Conservancy Council, which looks after the Beinn Eighe National Nature Reserve to the east. In this area, as in other parts of the Highlands, the red deer population has multiplied beyond the capacity of the environment to sustain it. The deer is a forest animal, but the forests that once provided food and shelter have largely disappeared. Today the deer compete for food, and do not get enough. The result is that Scotland's red deer are significantly smaller than their better-fed Continental cousins, and more susceptible to a hard winter, which can bring starvation and death.

The only way to control this situation is through culling, which is an important aspect of countryside management in most Highland areas. Culling is the rangers' task, and the policy is to take out about one-sixth of the population each year. It is the older and less fit animals that are culled, and the effect is to improve the stock and allow those that remain a greater chance of survival. It is part of the effort towards re-establishing the balance that has been disturbed by thousands of years of human activity.

South of Torridon are the Trust properties of Balmacara and Kintail, both acquired in the 1940s. Kintail is another tribute to the dedication of Percy Unna, who enabled the Trust to purchase it and add it to Glomach, the gift three years earlier of Mrs E C M Douglas and Lord Portman, proprietors of adjacent estates. The result was about 15,000 acres of mountain country, which include the famous Five Sisters and the impressive Falls of Glomach. Balmacara, on the peninsula lying between Loch Carron and Loch Alsh, looking towards Skye, was the bequest of Lady Hamilton. The two areas, characteristic of Highland scenery, with hills, sea lochs and rivers, are not many miles apart. They are linked through Loch Alsh and its offshoot Loch Duich, at the south-eastern end of which sits Kintail.

These properties add to the scope and variety of the Highland areas in the Trust's care. But Balmacara was almost lost. Following the discovery of oil in the North Sea there was an explosion of oil-related activity in the north and west of Scotland. In 1973 there was a proposal from the companies of Mowlem and Taylor Woodrow to construct twelve concrete platforms, which would rise 200 feet above sea level, at Port Cam, near Drumbuie in Balmacara. The tenants of sixteen croft holdings at Drumbuie objected, and in April 1973 the Trust announced its intention of lodging an objection. Balmacara was owned by the Trust 'inalienably'. Only an Act of Parliament could override that authority and enable construction to go ahead. But the Trust's action involved more than an attempt to protect its own property from some of the least acceptable consequences of development. A matter of principle was at stake which could affect many areas of coastal Scotland. The Trust made its policy clear:

> . . . *until it is proven by the Government that the scale of development necessary to service the oil industry can be integrated into the existing social fabric of the highlands, or that it is necessary in the national interest, the Trust and other bodies concerned with the protection of the environment must question the location of sites for large-scale oil-related development in the north-west.*

An appeal for funds met with considerable success and a public inquiry was duly held, early in 1974. The result was a victory for the local tenants and the Trust. The area was preserved and the inalienability of the Trust's ownership was upheld. This was important both as a statement of intent and of achievement. Although the Trust has not often had to fight major and expensive battles of this kind it demonstrated that it would and could, that it was a force to be reckoned with. The Seventies were a testing time for the environment, and the Trust played a key role, along with and often in partnership with many other organizations, in monitoring and controlling human activity, from the encroachment of industry to the encroachment of the apparently harmless tourist.

For tourism itself, which the Trust with its emphasis on welcoming the visitor with information and understanding has done so much to encourage, is a threat to the land. A watchful eye needs to be kept on visitors to Scotland's wild places and the provision for them. As urban pressures grow more intense, people seek the release that the countryside offers. An expanding interest in the natural environment, fostered by ecological concerns, means that increasing numbers want access to that environment. Percy Unna, who in the 1930s and '40s was dedicated to preserving the wilderness for the benefit of those relatively few who sought it out, could not have foreseen the extraordinary pilgrimage into the wild that is now such a striking feature of leisure and education.

The National Trust for Scotland has taken a lead in responding to this. The establishment of the ranger service was an important initiative, and the rangers have played a leading role in educating the public. But everywhere the countryside needs to be cared for. Vegetation and wildlife need to be protected and given space to flourish. The landscape itself, in danger of erosion by thousands of pairs of feet, has to be safeguarded. A large-scale project to restore damaged footpaths is now being undertaken, following an extensive report on the condition of paths on Trust and other mountainous properties. Without good footpaths walkers create new routes, which trample vegetation and hinder the painstaking work of encouraging growth and regeneration.

Many of the practical tasks involved in conservation are carried out by volunteers. Four local volunteer groups work with the Trust, and in addition there are the week-long Thistle Camps which run from spring to autumn at different Trust properties, and are open to anyone between the ages of seventeen and seventy. Volunteers carry out a range of work, such as tree-planting, refurbishing footpaths, clearance and drain-building, and also help with the restoration of buildings and dry stone dykes.

It is, of course, not only the magnificent Highland landscapes that need looking after. Amongst the Trust's properties are many other kinds of environment, stretches of coastline such as St Abb's Head, Berwickshire, protected habitats such as the wildfowl refuge at Threave, and farm and park land. An important part of the rangers' task is the monitoring of wildlife populations. At St Abb's Head, which came to the Trust in 1980 with the help of the Countryside Commission for Scotland, the Trust and the Scottish Wildlife Trust combine to monitor the populations of seabirds nesting there: this provides an insight into the wealth and productivity of the marine environment offshore. Since 1983 the area has been a National Nature Reserve. A year later Pearl Assurance Co Ltd gifted a further 167 acres of cliff and foreshore.

The underwater environment has received less attention than the land. To do something about this in the St Abbs area a committee was set up representing conservation groups, including the Trust, and local users. In 1984 the St Abbs and Eyemouth Voluntary Marine Nature Reserve was opened, its objective 'to conserve the outstanding biological richness of these inshore waters and to encourage responsible educational and recreational use alongside the traditional commercial fishery, to the mutual benefit of all'. The Reserve is wardened, and a code of practice has been devised. The Reserve continues to be managed as a collaborative effort.

Conservation and education go hand in hand. All over Scotland the Trust runs education programmes. As well as the network of visitor centres and ranger-guided walks there are numerous projects for the young. Scotland's first country park was opened at Culzean in 1969,

Kittiwake and razorbill on the rocks at St Abb's.

Cliffs at St Abb's.

and has over the years introduced thousands of youngsters to the resources of the countryside. Young Naturalists' Clubs are attached to a number of properties. Activity of this kind encourages both an awareness of the pleasures of the landscape, and a sensitivity towards its care. The lesson at the heart of it is that human survival depends on the survival of the natural environment, the foundation of Scotland's life, past, present and future.

CHAPTER TWO

The Shaping of the Nation

IN the timescale of the landscape people came late to Scotland, and the first arrivals did not stay long enough to create lasting settlements. They came, from Ireland, from England, from Scandinavia, to hunt on land and sea and gather shellfish. The earliest evidence of settlement dates from about 4000 BC, and thereafter for something like five thousand years men and women lived and died in Scotland with no, or very few, written accounts to record their activity. The records lie in the stones of their buildings, the imprint on the land, the valued objects that were placed in graves, and other artefacts that have survived decay. It is only relatively recent history that can be interpreted on the basis of evidence beyond what the archaeologists discover.

The evidence that is now in the care of the National Trust for Scotland is varied and extensive. It includes the traces left by ancient peoples and the more immediate records of our parents and grandparents. In between is an abundance of buildings and artefacts that help to map the course of Scotland's history. Evidence from a distance of several thousand years communicates as strongly as that speaking to us across a few decades. Often the years themselves lend power to the voices from the past, and the erosions of time encourage us to value what survives. But erosion can totally destroy, and it is the Trust's purpose to preserve, and to reinforce the value of rescue and conservation through interpretation.

There are areas of Scotland, now apparently barren and desolate, which once sustained vigorous communities. The rich scattering of cairns, brochs, stone circles and other relics hints at the millennia of existence. We can fill in a little of the detail, but much of it has to be surmise. In some ways we can discover more about attitudes to death than to life, for from neolithic times to the Viking invasions, which began around 800 AD, objects of significance and value were buried in graves. Burial places were themselves clearly important, special places marked in special ways. Amongst these are the Clava Cairns, near Inverness, which date from about 1600 BC, were gifted to the Trust by Alexander Munro of Leanach and are under the guardianship of the Historic Buildings and Monuments division of the Scottish Development Department. These consist of two chambered cairns and a ring-cairn, surrounded by standing stones. Stone endures, in a way that other building materials such as turf and wood do not. And it represents purpose and effort on the part of those who made use of it. At Clava, as at archaeological sites all over Scotland, we look at stones and think of people. Not far from the battlefield of Culloden, Clava is equally haunting in its effect.

The people who constructed the cairns farmed and hunted, were accomplished smiths and artists, and were involved in an extensive trade network. Sixteen hundred years later came outsiders who were to leave equally distinctive monuments, of a rather different kind. The Romans reached Scotland in AD 80. Although for three hundred years they controlled the southern part of Scotland, their presence was affected by the fluctuations of the Roman Empire in other parts of Europe. Initially they advanced to the River Tay and beyond, then settled in forts established in the Borders area before pulling back further south, to the line now marked by Hadrian's Wall, built in the 120s. Later, Hadrian's successor, Antoninus Pius, built another wall, from Bridgeness on the River Forth to Old Kilpatrick on the Clyde. Unlike Hadrian's Wall the Antonine Wall was made of turf on a stone foundation, and has not survived so well. But there are places where its remains are clearly detectable. Forts were built at two-mile intervals along the thirty-seven mile defence, to house garrisons of soldiers. Most of them can be identified, but the best preserved is Rough Castle, near Falkirk.

The Rough Castle site was originally excavated by the Society of Antiquaries of Scotland in 1903, and investigated again in the 1930s by Sir George Macdonald. It was established that the Wall must have been about ten feet high and fifteen feet wide at its base, with a defensive ditch dug in front of it, and a military road running behind it. It is probable that the need for the Wall was more symbolic than actual. It represented the authority of Rome and the imposition of stability. The Roman presence did bring peace and some economic benefits to the local populations as well as leaving the evidence of its three-hundred-year sojourn in the shape of remnants of buildings and many artefacts. Rough Castle came to the Trust in the 1930s, partly through gift, from Mr C W Forbes of Callander, and partly through purchase, and it is now in the guardianship of the Secretary of State.

The Antonine Wall was held for only about fifty years, and by 367 the Romans, under pressure from the Picts and other groups, abandoned their northern frontier. It might be argued that the Roman interlude in Scotland left a disproportionate quantity of evidence in relation to its long-term impact on Scotland's history. What happened in succeeding centuries probably shaped Scotland's future more forcefully. Nevertheless, Roman sites and Roman material have a particular fascination, and inevitably Roman artefacts were absorbed by the native population and influenced native craft workers.

The Romans were only one of many waves of invasion and influence that affected Scotland over the next few hundred years. The Teutonic Angles, the Irish Scots, later the Vikings and then the Anglo-Normans all contributed to the making of Scotland and the Scots. Scotland, so

Iona, with the abbey in centre background.

often characterized as remote from the mainstream of Europe, was a melting pot that drew its ingredients from many different sources. One of the most important of these was Ireland. From that small island came not only the people who were called Scots but one of two main sources of Scottish Christianity.

Christianity came to Britain with the Romans, but was driven into British (Welsh-speaking) areas by the Anglo-Saxon invaders. In Ireland it flourished, as the result of British missionaries, such as St Patrick. It was from Ireland that Columba came to Iona in 563, nearly two hundred years after Ninian, a Briton, had evangelized in the south and east of Scotland from his base at Whithorn. When Columba arrived from Ulster, Ninian's teachings had scarcely affected the west and Christianity had had little influence there. Columba was a Gaelic-speaking Scot, and he came to join his fellow-countrymen, who had raided Scotland and then settled after the withdrawal of the Romans. They occupied the area known as Dalriada, which corresponds approximately to modern Argyll.

From his base on Iona Columba spread the Christian message east and north, and also south to Northumbria. Iona became known not only as a centre of learning and religious faith, but also as a place of practical instruction and encouragement. It has ever since had a very special place in the consciousness of Scotland. After Columba's death in 597 the fortunes of the community on Iona were mixed. The island was raided successively by the Vikings, who destroyed the monastery and its outlying buildings. After a particularly devastating raid in 806, during which sixty-eight monks were murdered, the relics of Columba were divided and moved to Kells in Ireland and Dunkeld in Perthshire for safety. Later the monastery was rebuilt, only to be attacked again.

For several hundred years Iona continued to have a powerful religious magnetism, and was the preferred burial place of Scottish kings. In 1074 the monastery was restored by Queen Margaret, but as an Augustinian foundation, not as part of the Celtic church, which had faded with the acceptance of Rome as the centre of Christian authority. But the significance of Iona in the religious and cultural life of the western Highlands and the Hebrides did not fade. In the fifteenth century it became the seat of the Bishop of the Isles, and until the Reformation it had an influential presence, both symbolic and actual.

In 1899 the ecclesiastical buildings were given to the Church of Scotland by the eighth Duke of Argyll. Restoration of the abbey church followed, and its special nature was underlined by the stipulation in 1938 that all Christian denominations were welcome to worship there. Later some of the other buildings were restored, and they now house a Christian community. In 1980 the island of Iona, excluding the church buildings, was donated to the Trust as a gift to the nation in memory of the late Lord Fraser of Allander. This gave the Trust the responsibility for not only the land, resonant with religious and historical associations,

A croft on the island of Iona.

but a community. The island's 1,087 acres include two farms and fifteen crofts, and all the features of farming and crofting that these imply. It represents a striking fusion of the richness of past association and the practicalities of the present.

Kenneth McAlpin, who in the ninth century became ruler of a united kingdom north of the Forth and Clyde, was buried in Iona along with many other kings of Scotland, Ireland and Norway, including both Duncan and his rival Macbeth. When kings were no longer buried there it continued to have a strong association with island chiefs, which adds another layer of significance to the island.

But Iona was always vulnerable, and after the repeated Viking attacks the headquarters of the church were moved in the mid-ninth century to Dunkeld. The Trust's involvement with Dunkeld concerns the rebuilt town of the late seventeenth and early eighteenth centuries, but nevertheless Dunkeld's more ancient significance lingers. It was in the heart of Scotland, at a distance from its shores and from its southern border, all temptations to the invader. The distinctive features of the Columban church, with its spiritual emphasis, gave way to the more authority-based Roman church. Yet certain aspects of the Celtic way continued, and Iona itself has never lost its powerful association with the work and influence of St Columba.

The impact of the Vikings on Scotland was much more extensive than maraudings in the north and west. The need to resist and protect on the one hand, and to maintain alliances on the other, helped to strengthen the infant nation. The Vikings have left many traces, and not just the evidence of destruction. In the islands and Caithness and Sutherland particularly they established not only strongholds, but lasting communities, and Scotland became home for many who left Norway, which was finding it difficult to sustain a burgeoning population. Brodick Castle in Arran is on a site whose defensive potential was recognized by the Vikings. It gave them a bulwark in the Firth of Clyde, and although the signs of their occupation have long since been built over — for others saw the usefulness of the place — Brodick's Viking background is not forgotten.

Brodick Castle was accepted by the Treasury in 1958 in lieu of death duties on the estate of Lady Mary Hamilton, and the Trust then took on the responsibility of caring for it. Its oldest surviving remains date from the thirteenth century, by which time Scotland had both identity and cohesion as a nation. There was sufficient of both to absorb a degree of Anglo-Norman influence, and to resist, though at great cost, successive attempts at invasion. Invasion became more than a threat when the sudden death of Alexander III brought an unusually peaceful reign to an end. Edward I of England decided to take advantage of the confusion that resulted from the fact that there was no immediate heir to the throne. There were, however, several contenders, one of whom was

Looking across the battlefield and memorial rotunda at Bannockburn.

Robert Bruce, the grandfather of the future King Robert the Bruce, a figure whose presence lingers in and around many of the Trust's properties.

Edward invaded savagely in 1296, and was met by the vigorous resistance of William Wallace. But after ten years of harrying guerrilla warfare, Wallace was betrayed, captured and executed most horribly. A year later Bruce was proclaimed king. He continued the struggle with Edward, at first meeting defeat at Methven, and forced to go into hiding. He escaped to the west. After a period of refuge on Rathlin Island, off Northern Ireland, he was in Arran, where an unsuccessful attempt was made to dislodge the English, who were occupying Brodick Castle.

Brodick does not again come into the mainstream of Scottish history until the sixteenth century, but another Trust property represents a climax of the Bruce story, and has become a symbol of Scotland's independence. Part of the Bannockburn battlefield came to the Trust in 1932. In 1930 there were plans to build on it, and to resist this a committee had been formed under the tenth Earl of Elgin and Kincardine, the head of the Bruce family. Funds were raised and fifty-eight acres, which included the Borestone site where Bruce had his headquarters, were purchased. The ground was vested in the Trust, while the Battlefield Committee administered the site.

In spite of its highly symbolic significance sufficient funds were not raised to acquire the whole of the battlefield, but from the Borestone

Bannockburn: the commemorative statue of Robert the Bruce by Pilkington Jackson.

most of it can be seen. There, on June 23 and 24, 1314, one of the two most remembered battles in Scotland's history was fought. The victory at Bannockburn is regarded as a confirmation of the freedom and independence of the Scottish nation. After Bannockburn Scotland's identity was never in doubt, however much threatened. The second battle, at Culloden more than four hundred years later, has in a very different way strengthened Scottish identity. Both battlefields are in the care of the Trust, and both have been the focus of considerable efforts in conservation and interpretation.

King Robert's army, of about five and a half thousand men, faced and defeated an English army of nearly twenty thousand. The Scots were certainly helped by topography and by the over-confidence and lack of cohesion of the English side. Bruce himself acknowledged the crucial assistance of Angus Og Macdonald of Islay and his Highlanders, but this does not diminish his achievement as leader and general, nor his status as hero. Like Wallace he is vested with the symbolism of courageous resistance and national feeling. In the circumstances it is rather extraordinary that until Bannockburn came into the Trust's care nothing very much was done to preserve it or mark its significance. But from the 1950s in particular several developments have helped to maintain the battlefield and interpret it to the increasing numbers of visitors. In 1964 Her Majesty the Queen unveiled the now famous heroic statue by Pilkington Jackson, which had been commissioned by the King Robert the Bruce Memorial Committee. Three years later an information centre and auditorium were opened, and in 1972 an audio-visual presentation on the Wars of Independence, 'The Forging of a Nation', was launched.

Not surprisingly, Bannockburn has for many years been one of the most popular Trust properties with the public. For a few years the Scottish Tourist Board had an Information Centre at Bannockburn, but this was vacated in 1987, when the Trust mounted a new exhibition on 'The Kingdom of the Scots'.

The symbolism of Bannockburn is important for more than a victorious battle. The achievement of independence was advertised by the Declaration of Arbroath, six years later, as the independence not only of a nation and its ruler but of the individual: 'For it is not for riches, or honours, or glory that we fight, but for liberty alone, which no man loses save with his life.' And so it is right that the interpretation of Bannockburn should focus not just on how the battle was won, but also on what this meant for the Scottish nation.

Unfortunately, what it did not mean was peace. Much of Scottish history is the story of problems of succession. When Alexander III died his only direct heir was a three-year-old child Margaret, 'the Maid of Norway', whose death in turn unleashed contention and invasion. Robert's death in 1329 left a five-year-old, David II, as heir. The strife and confusion that followed allowed England to take frequent advantage. Over the next two hundred years even when there was no large-scale invasion, usually devastating if not disastrous for Scotland, there was almost constant border warfare. There were also bloody rivalries in the Highlands.

Yet Scotland not only survived but in many respects flourished, and many of the Trust's properties bear witness to this. Warfare or the threat of warfare brought a need for defences, and all over Scotland the homes of the powerful were built as defensive structures. From these strongholds raids were conducted and invasion resisted. Many are now in ruins. Others were incorporated into new and 'modern' buildings, which represented the power of wealth rather than of arms. The original castle at Culzean, for example, was one of several small fortified residences belonging to the Kennedy family. It was a characteristic tower house in a commanding position on a cliff top. From it and their other castles the Kennedys dominated for several centuries a wide area south from the Firth of Clyde. It was not in itself a particularly significant building, but in the eighteenth century the old tower house was rebuilt. The new castle is one of the finest achievements of the architect Robert Adam, but there is nothing remaining of the modest fortified house it once was.

Drum Castle, however, still preserves its splendid thirteenth-century keep. Drum, ten miles west of Aberdeen, was taken on by the Trust in 1976. It came as a bequest, with an endowment, from Henry

Drum Castle.

Forbes Irvine: the castle had been the home of the Irvines since the time of Robert the Bruce. In 1323 Bruce granted the charter of the Royal Forest of Drum to his armour-bearer William de Irwin. William had been a loyal follower of Bruce for many years; his home near Dumfries was close to the original Scottish home of the Bruce family. (The Bruces had come to Scotland as part of the Norman incursion encouraged by David I, who hoped that an imported feudal system might help to control his volatile kingdom.)

By the time William de Irwin came to Drum the seventy-feet high keep was probably already built, for its walls seem to date from before 1290. They may have been the work of Richard Cementarius, master mason to Alexander III, repairer of the subsequently destroyed castle of Aberdeen, and Aberdeen's first provost. Both William the Lion and Alexander III hunted in the Forest of Drum, and there was probably a hunting lodge there. But the keep itself, with walls more than twelve feet thick, suggests a defensive purpose, and the representation of royal authority. A fortress was a way of signalling a strong presence: Robert I's gift to William rewarded his loyalty, but also showed his dependence on his supporters.

For more than six hundred years Drum Castle remained in the Irwin, or Irvine, family. It was besieged and occupied more than once, and around it eddied much dramatic incident, typical of the contentions of the times. Feuding, rivalries and outright warfare were the dominant features. In 1411 the Battle of Harlaw, the 'Reid Harlaw' as it was called, on account of its bloodiness, was fought twenty miles north of Drum. The third laird, Sir Alexander Irvine, fought in the army raised by the Earl of Mar to oppose the invasion of Donald, Lord of the Isles, who was laying claim to the Earldom of Ross. Donald was halted, but in the course of the battle Alexander engaged in single combat with Maclean of Duart, known as Red Hector of the Battles. Both men were killed. Both the struggle itself and the result can be seen as an emblem of the divisions that have played so formidable a role in Scotland's history.

In a variety of ways Drum and the Irvine family were leading actors both on the local stage and in the affairs of the nation. The fourth laird was in 1424 instrumental in obtaining the release of James I, captured by the English in 1406 as a boy of eleven. The sixth laird was rewarded by James V for his peace-keeping operations against 'rebels, thieves, robbers, reivers, sorcerers and murderers'. Twenty years later his son was killed at the battle of Pinkie. Later Irvines fought at Sheriffmuir and at Culloden.

Throughout the fourteenth and fifteenth centuries the Scottish kings had to cope with interference and provocation from England. The Scottish barons were contentious and difficult, challenging each other's power and that of the king. In the fifteenth and sixteenth centuries a series of minorities left the monarchy vulnerable. In such circumstances the stronghold of Drum, and others like it, had a particular importance. With the seventeenth century came a period of relative stability, before Scotland was disrupted by the wars of the 1640s and '50s. The castle as it now stands is largely the result of its extension in 1619, but although this produced a handsome Jacobean mansion the keep remains as a rugged reminder of earlier uncertain times.

Not far away from Drum is Crathes Castle which, although not built until the sixteenth century, also has indirect connections with Robert the Bruce. The Burnett family, like the Bruces, came originally from England, but their origins were Anglo-Saxon rather than Norman. Alexander Burnard, as the name was then, was rewarded, as William de Irwin had been, for his loyalty to Bruce. He was given an estate at Banchory and the post of Royal Forester of Drum. There was no splendid castle or fortification for him to occupy. Instead, the Burnetts made their home in a crannog, a prehistoric man-made island, in the Loch of the Leys, and remained there for 250 years. Although they, like the Irvines, were involved in events both local and national — the son of Alexander fought with Mar at Harlaw — they avoided the worst effects of centuries of strife. Slowly the family's fortunes rose, and land and wealth were acquired through marriage. By the sixteenth century it was felt the time had come to leave their island stronghold and build a more prestigious residence. The castle that was to be called Crathes was begun in the middle of the sixteenth century, and was one of the last major houses to be built in a vernacular style unaffected by the growing

The Library — the original High Hall of the old keep — at Drum Castle with a portrait of Hugh Irvine as the Archangel Gabriel.

foreign influences. Like Drum, it was to be lived in for many generations by the same family, until it came to the Trust in 1951 as the bequest of Sir James Burnett of Leys.

Almost due north of Crathes lies the castle of Fyvie, eight miles south-east of Turriff. Fyvie, too, is a reminder of those tumultuous centuries when Scotland's kings were trying to consolidate their power. Although there was probably an earlier timber structure, the castle itself dates from the fourteenth century. It was first held by the crown, and like Drum had its origins in the royal interest in hunting and the need for a foothold in the north. William the Lion and Alexander III were both at Fyvie. So was Edward I, in 1296. Some years later Robert the Bruce held an open-air court in the Fyvie beech woods.

In the first decades of its existence this massive fortification passed through several hands, instances of the power-broking through which control of Scotland was sought. Robert II presented it to his son the Earl of Carrick, later Robert III. He gave the castle to his cousin, Sir James Lindsay, Lord of Crawford and Buchan, from whom it went to Sir Henry Preston as part of a ransom deal for an English knight, Ralph de Percy, who was captured at the Battle of Otterburn in 1388. It then passed, through marriage, to the Meldrum family, who in 1596 sold Fyvie to Alexander Seton. Fyvie changed hands several more times until finally, in 1984, funds generously provided by the National Heritage Memorial Fund enabled the Trust to purchase and endow the castle.

The original purpose of Fyvie was to provide a strong presence at the edge of the Grampians, a means of holding some of the less tameable elements in Scotland's powerful families. The original structure has been overlaid by successive centuries of addition and extension, and the castle and its contents are rich in evidence of many times and several families, whose fortunes have been very varied. Yet something of its early character remains, and the links with the crucial events of the thirteenth and fourteenth centuries survive.

The beginnings of Kellie Castle, three miles from Pittenweem in Fife, reach back even further, to the eleventh century, when Siward, probably a relation of the Siward who was Earl of Northumbria and Saxon in origin, acquired Kellie. Eventually the castle came to Sir Walter Oliphant, who married Elizabeth, a daughter of Robert the Bruce. In 1562 the Kellie estates, by this time extensive, were sold to another branch of the family, Lawrence, third Lord Oliphant.

The oldest part of the existing castle probably dates back to the fourteenth century. In 1573 the fourth Lord Oliphant married Lady Margaret Hay, and the date is commemorated on the new tower he built at this time, at a distance from the original keep. This rather odd arrangement was later resolved, with the building of a third tower, and the linking of the three together. The result is a much less vertical structure than the traditional fortified house, and gives Kellie a quality

Kellie Castle and gardens.

that is both individual and firmly within the Scottish vernacular idiom. Its later history fostered its distinctive character, especially when it was owned and cared for by the Lorimer family of architects and artists. Kellie was purchased by the Trust in 1970 with the help of the National Land Fund, the Pilgrim Trust and an anonymous donation, but the purchase was only possible with additional support of funds for an endowment, a large part of which came from the same anonymous donor.

Fife escaped the worst ravages of Scotland's journey to nationhood, being neither centre stage nor on the vulnerable peripheries. It is the Aberdeenshire castles that remind us that Scotland's struggle for identity did not end with Bannockburn. That was, in fact, a beginning. Each of these castles is an accumulation of layers of evidence and meaning. Their stories go back more than six hundred years, encouraging us to uncover the centuries that they have witnessed. Buildings are marvellously evocative, because they contain the histories of places as well as of families, and have associations with individuals, known and unknown, as well as with great events. Their contents augment a story which will always remain tantalisingly incomplete, but which is almost the richer for the margins of uncertainty.

They are huge responsibilities, for the Trust's proprietorship is a commitment both to conservation and to assisting our appreciation of the past. These are tasks which involve a continuous vigilance, and a sensitive understanding of the buildings and their context. They also involve an assessment of what is appropriate and achievable in terms of restoration and preservation, and this is very much the responsibility of the Trust's curators. The Trust has its own workshops, where a great deal of the conservation and reconstruction work on artefacts and fittings is carried out, and also goes to craftsmen outside when additional expertise is needed. The result of skilled craftsmanship and attention to detail is the sustaining of an environment authentic to its period and the way of life that shaped it.

This created environment is part of our tangible link with the continuum of Scotland's life and character. The identity of the Scottish nation was affected from the outset by the rugged and demanding nature of the landscape, and by the toughness and determination of the people, from saints to soldiers. The cairns and castles, abbeys and battlefields, are eloquent reinforcements of our understanding of this.

CHAPTER THREE

Castles and Culture

THE castles and fortified houses of Scotland were witnesses to troubled times. Gradually their character changed, and their evolution reflected shifts in Scottish life and society. They became less a means of defence and of the imposition of authority, more emblems of stability and influence. But during most of the two and a half centuries of the Stewart kings, the governing of Scotland continued to be a hazardous and turbulent business. There were threats to security within the nation, and tenacious enemies without. Kingship was precarious, for although the Stewart dynasty itself was never challenged, individual monarchs were surrounded by violent rivalries amongst Scottish barons. Some of Scotland's kings were sucked into these disputes and destroyed by them.

The Stewart rulers seemed dogged by ill-luck. The line was in direct descent from Robert II, son of Robert the Bruce's daughter Marjory, who married Walter, sixth High Steward, but after Robert III there was not a single monarch who was of age when he or she inherited. Each of the first three Jameses was a young boy when he became king. James IV was sixteen, and his son James and his granddaughter Mary were infants when their fathers died. With this succession of youthful rulers the way was open for power struggles between rival factions. And the old enemy, England, was rarely quiet for long.

Border raiding was almost incessant, and the Highlands remained untamed, if anything an arena of increasing bloodshed. Border barons and Highland chieftains could pose difficult problems of politics and power. Yet, while the kingdom was often in turmoil and the story of kingship and government is punctuated with betrayal and murder, jealousy and conflict, Scotland's strength and character as a nation developed. Trade, in particular with northern Europe, expanded and flourished, and ports, small as well as large, became busy and prosperous. The burghs, first instituted by David I, were focal points of trade and manufacture, and played a crucial role in the nation's growing prosperity. Their importance is illustrated in some of the small towns in which the Trust has an involvement through the Little Houses Improvement Scheme, for example Culross and Dysart. Although the houses the Trust has been instrumental in restoring are of a later date, the communities themselves became significant under the Stewart kings.

Commercial and cultural activities continued purposefully through political turbulence. James I, skilled in the martial arts, certainly an asset in disordered Scotland, was also a poet and musician. He brought a period of firm government to the country, and a sensitivity towards the arts, but he treated his Stewart kinsmen viciously and his end was violent. He was horribly murdered in 1436 while staying in a convent in Perth.

The Scottish nobles naturally took advantage of James II's minority to pursue power for themselves. Later, James had no difficulty in asserting himself, but he too died violently, though accidentally, by an exploding cannon. But he had succeeded in taking over the earldom of Mar in the north-east, and established control by settling his people on its lands. He was an astute king, who carefully arranged alliances and created peers as a means of consolidating his position. A beneficiary was Thomas Fraser, who was granted the barony of Muchall and Stoneywood, once a part of the lands of Mar.

Thomas Fraser came from Stirling but, like the Bruces, the Irvines and the Burnetts, all families linked with Trust properties in the north-east, the Frasers had settled in the Scottish Lowlands in the twelfth century. Thomas was a loyal supporter of James, and Muchall and Stoneywood were his reward, granted in 1454 in exchange for his lands near Stirling. The granting of lands and titles was the customary pattern of encouraging loyalty, and lands in particular were a necessary economic base for those ambitious for power.

It is likely that Thomas Fraser built the stone keep at Dunecht that was the nucleus of Castle Fraser, but there may have been an earlier structure. The Fraser family flourished, although after James II's death the country was again unsettled. His son, James III, was less effective in maintaining order. The barons despised and took advantage of his interest in artistic and intellectual pursuits. His encouragement of music and poetry did not protect him from a violent death. He was thrown from his horse in flight from rebellious Border barons who confronted him at Sauchieburn, and stabbed while incapacitated by his fall.

By the middle of the fourteenth century there were in the north-east a string of castles, for the most part formidable and uncompromising, which protected landowners and held down potential disturbance. The Frasers became part of this network, strengthening their position through marriage with other powerful families in the area, including the Irvines of Drum. In the 1570s the fifth laird, Michael Fraser, planned the rebuilding of the castle. By 1576 work was under way. A square tower was constructed, linked with a great hall, possibly the original building, with a round tower attached to the diagonally opposite corner: a common design for fortified buildings often described as a Z-plan.

The first stages of the work were carried out by a local stonemason, Thomas Leiper. His son James also worked on the castle, and a member of another noted Aberdeenshire family of masons, John Bell, was responsible for later work. John Bell's father had built Midmar, a Z-plan castle in the area which probably influenced the design of Castle

Castle Fraser.

Fraser. The contribution of the stone itself to the character of the Grampian castles cannot be overemphasized, and the masons' skill in handling the material was central to their success. It is the stone that gives them their forthright solidity, which is yet organic to the landscape.

Michael Fraser died before work on the castle was completed, but his son Andrew took up the task with enthusiasm. With the completion of the external work attention was turned to the interior, and to the building of the servants' quarters as well as the kitchen, bakehouse and brewhouse. By 1633, when Andrew was created first Lord Fraser, there was in existence a new home, entirely fitting for his new status. Like most of Scotland's prominent families the Frasers were unable to escape the contentions of the seventeenth century, but for a few years

Lord Fraser was able to enjoy in relative peace the splendid turreted, gabled structure that emerged after a century of building activity.

Castle Fraser came to the Trust in 1976, when it was gifted by Major and Mrs Michael Smiley, the granddaughter of Viscount Cowdray who had bought the castle in 1921. Although there were later alterations and much of the interior reflects later styles part of the castle still retains its sixteenth-century character, particularly the square Michael Tower and the Great Hall. The removal of the external harling has revealed the texture of the stone again. The Trust has retained the individuality of the different phases in the castle's history, for example in the replacement of fittings and wallpaper and the re-weaving from an old pattern of one of the bedroom carpets. As with the other castles of medieval origin in the Trust's care this preservation of layers of history has been an important part of the restoration.

At Fyvie, not far away, changes were also in progress. Alexander Seton, later to become Chancellor of Scotland, bought the castle, eight miles from Turriff, in 1596. He enlarged it, and added the distinctive bartizans, dormers and decorative finials, which give the building such a theatrical character. This flamboyance did not reflect the fortunes of the family, however, for the Setons did not continue to flourish. Alexander's grandson supported the Jacobites, and was involved in the 1689 resistance to King William. He died in Paris in 1694, a penniless exile.

Further south there was a happier story at Crathes, near Banchory. Alexander Burnett fought for James III just months before the king was murdered. His reward was Banchory as a free barony. A connection was forged with the church when a later Alexander married Janet Hamilton, daughter of the Canon of Arbroath, in 1543. She brought church land with her, and the useful friendship of David Beaton, Archbishop of Arbroath. Three years later the Archbishop was murdered, by zealots resentful of both his close relations with France and his somewhat worldly outlook, but by that time the Burnetts had benefited in wealth and influence.

The decades which saw the Burnett family growing in substance and fortune were troubled times for Scotland. Yet it was felt appropriate to initiate the building of a new home, which would be a symbol of the Burnetts' new position. The castle at Crathes was begun in 1553. It was not a time favourable for building. Scotland yet again had a child monarch, this time the young Mary, Queen of Scots. Her grandfather James IV had been a popular and effective ruler, but he did not crack the problem of the English, and died at their hands at the tragically pointless battle of Flodden. Her father James V dealt ruthlessly with those in his own kingdom who posed a threat, but war with England again deflected efforts at strong government. It was after the defeat of the Scots by the English at Solway Moss in 1542 that James died, aged only thirty-one.

Crathes Castle.

His baby daughter Mary was taken to France, and when work began on the Burnetts' new castle she was still there. Nine years later the castle at Crathes was not finished and the Burnetts still occupied their island home, but by that time Mary had returned to Scotland and was trying to bring her contentious country, now affected by the additional divisions of religion, under control. This involved doing battle with the Earl of Huntly at Corrichie, very close to the Loch of the Leys. Alexander Burnett fought in her victorious army, commanded by the Earl of Mar.

Alexander died in 1574 and neither his son nor his grandson lived for many years after. By the time Crathes was ready for occupation, twenty years later, it was the great-grandson of the man who actually initiated the building, another Alexander, who moved in. Even then there was still work going on. The interior was not completed until 1602, the last year in which a Stewart was king of Scotland only. The project took half a century to complete, and that half century saw far-reaching changes, in government, in allegiances, and in the foundations of religious belief.

The construction of the castle was probably the work of the same John Bell who was involved in the extensions at Castle Fraser, and he gave Crathes many of the characteristic features of the earlier fortified houses, though these are more decorative than functional. The idiom was appropriate, while the defensive purpose was no longer important. The century that was greeted by the completion of Crathes would not be a peaceful one, but the clashes were no longer caused by baronial

Restoring a painted ceiling at Crathes Castle.

Part of the 'Nine Nobles' ceiling at Crathes, after restoration.

The Horn of the Leys, Crathes Castle. The original horn, presented to Alexander Burnard by Robert the Bruce, is displayed in the castle.

The Green Lady's Room, Crathes Castle.

rivalries. And the nature of warfare was itself changing, which made castles less strongholds of military significance and more symbols of proprietorship and authority.

Alexander Burnett was a man of considerable education and had lively cultural interests. This is reflected in the enthusiasm with which he embarked on decorating the interior of Crathes. The full extent of this decoration was for many years obliterated, until in 1877 it was discovered that underneath layers of eighteenth-century lathe and plaster were beautiful tempera-painted ceilings. The techniques of tempera painting had their origins in the early thirteenth century. They involved mixing pigments with glues or egg yolk, which gave particularly fresh and vivid colours. Tempera was a favourite medium for painting on wood panelling.

Scots had become acquainted with painted wood ceilings in

Scandinavia and the Baltic, and imported the idea along with large quantities of timber from these areas. The beams and planks of the ceiling were painted after they were in place, so the size, shape and spacing of the wood to some extent dictated the subject. The outline of the design was drawn in black on a background painted in a mixture of chalk and size. The colours were then painted in. The whole process required meticulous artistry and considerable time.

Alexander chose for his ceiling the theme of the Nine Nobles — nine heroes of legend and history. It was a favourite design, which may have been taken from Continental pattern books, although the painters themselves were probably Scottish. Today the nine heroes, Hector, Julius Caesar, Alexander the Great, King David, Joshua, Judas Maccabeus, King Arthur, Charlemagne and Godfrey de Bouillon, look down with a lively and appealing presence, but they were close to being lost for ever. Their survival represents one of the Trust's most remarkable conservation achievements. In 1959, eight years after Crathes came to the Trust, a Gulbenkian Foundation grant made it possible to provide specialist training for a restorer. Ian Hodkinson spent some time researching in Scandinavia before undertaking the task of restoration. To accomplish this the ceiling was removed to conservation workshops at Stenhouse Mansion in Edinburgh, where it was worked on intensively for several months. The job involved the careful consolidation of the old flaking paint, which was often only possible under a magnifying glass. A second painted ceiling has also survived, in the room now known as the 'Green Lady's Room', after a female figure who is said to haunt the castle with a child in her arms.

Stenhouse Mansion, which is now leased to the Scottish Development Department, came to the Trust in 1938 as a gift from the Greyhound Racing Association. It had been the home of a seventeenth-century Edinburgh merchant, Patrick Ellis, who added to the sixteenth-century house in 1623. It now houses the SDD Restoration Centre, which carries out a range of conservation work for its own and the Trust's properties.

Alexander Burnett enjoyed seventeen years of the completed Crathes. By the time of his death in 1619 the direction of Scotland's history had changed. With the imprisonment of Mary in 1567 by Queen Elizabeth of England, Scotland had another child monarch, her son James. But in 1603 James VI became ruler of both kingdoms, and the centre of government shifted to London. The castles of Aberdeenshire were a long way from the southern capital, but they were not beyond the reach of the major upheavals that were so much a feature of that century.

The west coast of Scotland was less in the mainstream of political activity, but still vulnerable. On the island of Arran Brodick Castle had been exposed both to attack and to political manipulation. The castle was stormed by the English in 1406 and by the Lord of the Isles in 1455. In 1467 Princess Mary, sister of the sixteen-year-old James III, married

Sir Thomas Boyd of the family in whose charge the young king was. Sir Thomas was duly created Earl of Arran. But James himself was not happy with the marriage, and two years later he stripped Sir Thomas of his earldom and insisted on his sister's divorce and remarriage, to James, Lord Hamilton. In 1503 James Hamilton, son of this second marriage, was created Earl of Arran by James IV.

The new earl began extensions to Brodick Castle, perhaps hoping to strengthen his position close to the throne as well as the building. But in 1529 it was again attacked, in the feuding over who should have controlling influence over the young James V. History was repeated when the second Earl of Arran was appointed Regent to the infant Mary, Queen of Scots. In this position he arranged with Henry VIII of England the betrothal of Mary to Henry's son Edward, heir to the throne. When the arrangement was rejected by the Scots, Henry angrily invaded Scotland, and the Earl of Lennox, Arran's enemy, destroyed Brodick. In 1558 Brodick was burned again, this time by the English. Over the centuries it received more batterings than any other property now looked after by the Trust.

The Earl of Arran continued in the role of marriage broker, and was awarded the dukedom of Chatelherault by Henry II of France for the part he played in negotiating the betrothal of Mary and Henry's son, Francis. But Hamilton's ambitions for power backfired and lost them their lands and titles. It was not until 1599, with James VI on the throne, that the family was restored to favour, with the award first of the title of marquess, and some decades later of duke.

Although its politics were turbulent, Stewart Scotland was culturally extremely vigorous, especially in the reigns of James IV and V. This was the result both of native artistry and of an openness to outside influences. In spite of the enmity with England there was some receptivity to English ideas. Trade with northern Europe brought cultural as well as commercial exchange: the vogue for painted ceilings is an example. But the most striking influence came from France. The sixteenth century saw a revival of the Auld Alliance, which had originated with a treaty between Scotland and France in 1295. Relations had fluctuated, but now the influence of French ideas in art and architecture was being distinctly felt in Scotland. A leading illustration of this influence is Falkland Palace.

There had been a stronghold at Falkland, in Fife, since at least the twelfth century. In the thirteenth century it was the castle of the Macduffs, earls of Fife. In the 1450s James II gave Falkland to his wife Mary of Gueldres, and there followed its transformation into a royal residence. It was a place to escape to from the cares of government and the pressures of power. Now only the outline remains of the great hall which James built there. Between 1500 and 1513 James IV enlarged the hall and extended the East Range of the palace. James V was a prisoner at Falkland as a boy, but that did not prejudice him against the

Falkland Palace (overleaf).

Palace. On the contrary, it became a particular centre of interest.

In 1536 James V took up the work of extending and renovating Falkland Palace. He employed French and Scottish masons to provide the building with an elegant dressed stone facing. The style is of the French Renaissance, and was a tribute to the close relationship with France cemented by James's two marriages, to Princess Madeleine of France who died soon after coming to Scotland, and then to Mary of Guise.

The calculated ruthlessness that James employed in his efforts to impose his power on the kingdom was effective, but at a heavy price, for several nobles suffered who seem to have posed little threat. One of these was Sir James Hamilton of Finnart, architect of improvements to royal palaces at Linlithgow, Stirling, Edinburgh and Falkland. Although he executed its architect (Sir James was also his cousin), Falkland became the king's favourite residence. It was to Falkland that he went in December 1542, defeated and broken after the disaster at Solway Moss. The news that the queen had given birth to a daughter at Linlithgow Palace was probably little consolation: his comment was that the Stewart line would 'gang wi' a lass'. This was more realistic as a premonition of his own end, for he died a few days later, while his daughter survived not only to be queen, but to bear a son who would become king of both England and Scotland.

Falkland Palace still retains a character of elegance that indicates its function not as a place of government, with which Edinburgh and Stirling were identified, but as a place of relaxation. James V added a classical flavour to the buildings, with two French masons in charge of the work. The first, Moise Martyne, died at Falkland in 1538. The following year Nicholas Roy arrived, and continued the work of adding buttresses and medallions which contribute to the Palace's suggestion

The Keeper's Bedroom, Falkland Palace.

Carved woodwork on the James VI four-poster bed in the Keeper's Bedroom, Falkland Palace.

CASTLES AND CULTURE

Anyone for Royal Tennis? Falkland Palace.

The Royal Tennis Court, Falkland Palace.

of a French château. Yet the work was not completed, and there is no obvious explanation for the fact that building ceased in 1541, more than a year before James's death. The East Range is now a ruin, possibly the victim of careless Cromwellian soldiers who accidentally started a fire. But the South Range still stands, modest in scale and harmonious in aspect.

Falkland offered a respite from city noise and crowds — even in the sixteenth century Edinburgh was notoriously congested and unsalubrious. Falkland was a haven where the country activities of hunting and hawking provided entertainment, and the gentler pursuits of music and dancing were favourite ways of passing the time indoors. The surrounding forest still offered game, although it had been raided to provide timber for James IV's prized warship the *Great Michael*. From 1535 its trees were protected by Act of Parliament. The timber for

Detail of the decorated ceiling, the Chapel Royal, Falkland Palace.

James V's renovations came from the Baltic and Scandinavia, like that for the building of Crathes. It was James V who had a tennis court built at Falkland, so that he and his courtiers could enjoy the game that was another import from France. The Falkland court, restored in the 1890s, is the oldest in Britain. The original game, called Royal or Real Tennis to distinguish it from lawn tennis which came later, is a more complicated game than its relative.

The king moved from place to place with a huge entourage, receiving from the tenants on royal lands rents paid in kind which provisioned his household. Thus his visits to Falkland were motivated by a combination of pragmatism and pleasure. The palace filled with the king, his family, the court, and a very large number of servants and retainers. A few weeks stay strained resources considerably, both to feed the company and deal with the unsanitary accumulation of waste and smells. Then it would be time for the king to move on to another royal residence, or to take advantage of aristocratic hospitality.

Mary, Queen of Scots also used Falkland as a country retreat, and initiated some repairs there. Mary was at Falkland when the Earl of Arran, son of the earl who was Regent when she was a child, and the Earl of Bothwell made an attempt to abduct her. Arran's intention was to marry Mary, who was now a widow — the question of Mary's marriage was of considerable political and religious interest. He ended his life in prison, and later Mary married Bothwell. Two years after Mary's death in 1587 her son James married Anne of Denmark and Falkland Palace again became a gift to a bride. But it did not remain a haven of peace, for not only were there wrangles about the entitlement to the land around the Palace but in 1592 it was attacked by another Earl of Bothwell, in reaction against James VI's accusations that he was guilty of witchcraft. The attack was unsuccessful, but it underlined the continuing vulnerability of Scotland's rulers.

Falkland Palace, which has been in the care of Trust since 1952, owes part of its character to the fact that it fronts the street of the burgh. It is not a 'great house' set apart from the community, but a residence fitting in with the scale of the rest of the town. The Trust's involvement with the burgh of Falkland echoes this close relationship. Seven buildings have been renovated through the Little Houses Improvement Scheme. In 1986 the Trust bought the Town Hall, built in 1800, which now houses an exhibition on local history which complements the Palace. The fortunes of the burgh were closely linked with the Palace, with several members of the court having houses there. During royal visits those for whom there was no room in the Palace found lodgings in the town, and the local economy was very much geared to feeding and servicing the royal household.

After James VI's departure to England Falkland's place in the Scottish scene faded. James returned to Scotland only once, in 1617, and although on that occasion he did fit in a visit to Falkland his

The Chapel Royal, Falkland Palace.

attachment to Scotland in general and to Falkland in particular was not strong enough to bring him back. When James's son Charles I came to Scotland in 1633 he also stayed in the Palace. Charles II was at Falkland in 1650, when he was in Scotland for his coronation at Scone, in defiance of Cromwell's government, and again in 1651. Cromwell had entered Scotland, but Scottish support for the Crown was strong. It was at Falkland that Charles made the decision to march into England. He gathered an army and headed south, not realizing that Cromwell, far from being caught unaware, was allowing him to penetrate deep into England before catching and defeating him at Worcester.

Charles did not return to Scotland, let alone to Falkland, after his restoration to the throne. Falkland's days as a royal retreat were over, and during the next 150 years the Palace crumbled into a semi-ruinous state. It was in the charge of hereditary Keepers but remained, and remains, the property of the Crown. In 1887 the Falkland estates were bought by Patrick Crichton Stuart, third Marquess of Bute, whose considerable historical interests involved him in numerous restoration projects. Falkland was no exception. With the purchase of the estates he became hereditary Keeper of the Palace, and set about reclaiming the neglected buildings. He initiated an ambitious process of restoration, which was carried on by his successors, Lord Ninian Crichton Stuart (the third Marquess's second son) and his son Michael Crichton Stuart. It was the latter, and his wife Barbara, who, with the garden designer Percy Cane, was responsible for work on the grounds, which involved restoring the main gardens on the basis of a seventeenth-century plan. The Keepership continues with this junior branch of the Bute family.

In 1952 Major Michael Crichton Stuart, Hereditary Constable, Captain and Keeper of Falkland Palace, appointed the National Trust for Scotland as Deputy Keeper of the Palace. At the same time an endowment was provided to enable the maintenance of the palace and garden. The Trust continued with the task of rehabilitation and interior decoration which had been begun by the third Marquess. In the king's bedchamber traditional windows and a timber ceiling were installed, in keeping with a style that would have been familiar to James V. The splendid golden bed which can now be seen there is of slightly later date, but the room, with its painted ceiling and frieze and hanging tapestries, is an evocative reminder of Falkland's heyday.

The history that moved away from Falkland in the seventeenth century has been recovered and kept alive, in both the Palace and the town. 1989 saw the 450th anniversary of the Royal Tennis Court, which was commemorated by an exhibition describing the game and its history, and an international Royal Tennis Tournament. The exhibition was opened by His Royal Highness the Prince Edward, who followed the more formal part of his visit with a game on the court which was once played on by his Stewart forebears.

CHAPTER FOUR

Miners, Mariners and Merchants

HE dramatic political events of sixteenth-century Scotland directly affected life in many of the great houses, and through those the Trust maintains this is vividly focused. Beneath the public surface the country prospered in some striking respects, although much of Scotland remained poor, especially in the eyes of visitors from richer countries, such as southern England. Three quarters of the population struggled at a level of basic subsistence, as they did in most other European countries. But Scotland was by contemporary standards a fairly typical and moderately prosperous northern European land. There were many small and active trading burghs and overseas trade was expanding.

The involvements of the National Trust for Scotland illustrate some of the features of Scotland's commercial success and prosperity. The homes of merchants and burgesses were echoing in a more modest fashion some of the features that were being introduced in the great houses. Dining and drawing rooms reflected social refinement. Those who could afford it panelled their rooms with wood and used silk and leather for furnishings. Glass and silver on the dinner table were further signs of growing commercial success. And as commercial enterprise brought a degree of economic stability it also became linked with a stronger political voice. By the early sixteenth century, with the decades of relative quiet brought by the reign of James VI and I, the home of a successful merchant was a place of substance and wellbeing. Its display of both imported goods, wood panelling, carpets and tapestries perhaps, and local craftsmanship, linen damask, silver and glass from the factories encouraged by James, revealed a growing taste for comfort and even elegance.

Aberdeen was a city that benefited from the developments in trade, although it had long since established its identity as an active commercial centre. Its success stemmed from its independent relationship with the Continent of Europe, particularly Scandinavia, with which it had pursued a vigorous trade. Aberdeen's importance was recognized by a succession of monarchs, and an exemption from tolls encouraged merchants. A stream of commodities passed through Aberdeen's port: hides, wool, meal, salt and cured fish, especially salmon. Aberdeen's fisheries were one of the burgh's most significant sources of wealth. In 1286 Aberdeen had a population of about 1400. By the middle of the sixteenth century the town had grown to accommodate 4000, and the countryside round about sustained numerous landowning families, some of whose lives, like the Irvines of

Craigievar Castle.

Drum, had become closely associated with Aberdeen's history. The city was impressive, in aspect and in economic success, and the poet William Dunbar, a visitor in 1511, celebrated Aberdeen as 'the lamp of beautie, bountie and blythness'.

Aberdeen escaped none of the major movements and changes in Scotland as a whole, but the people of the town dealt pragmatically with the encroachment of political and religious upheaval. Their pragmatism probably contributed to Aberdeen's success, and if her position at a distance from the centre of intrigue and contention was not a protection at least it meant minimal interference with her development. By the sixteenth century a small community of thatched, timber-framed buildings was being transformed into a more solid and extended stone-built city. In 1604 permission was granted to one John the Mason to excavate a quarry to provide building stones for a growing demand. On several occasions in the past Aberdeen, like many Scottish towns, had been devastated by fire. Building in stone was a move towards permanence.

Amongst the stone-built domestic dwellings that went up in the sixteenth century was the house in Shiprow, built possibly by Andrew Jamesone, mason, in 1593. Jamesone was the father of George Jamesone, the first Scottish portrait painter of any note, who also provided plans for the town's first public park. The original owners of the house may have been Robert Watson, wright, and his wife Margaret Collie, or Alexander Farquhar. Now the second oldest domestic building in 'New' Aberdeen, it is known as Provost Ross's house. Provost John Ross, a successful merchant, became owner of the house in 1702. He put in a new front door so that he could look out over the harbour and derive satisfaction from the sight of his own ships.

The Trust acquired Provost Ross's house in 1952, when it was threatened with demolition, and restored it with the financial support of Aberdeen Town Council. Her Majesty Queen Elizabeth the Queen Mother, Patron of the National Trust for Scotland, played an instrumental role in the rescue of the house with an adroit word after a visit to Aberdeen. The house retains a number of original features, including beam-and-board ceilings on the ground floor, and the restoration has been in sympathy with its original character. It now houses the Aberdeen Maritime Museum, which includes a highly appropriate evocation of an Aberdeen ship-owning family. Its links with Aberdeen's trading and shipping heritage are reinforced by its nearness to the sights and sounds of the harbour.

In 1963 a local consortium raised the money to buy a building that has been described as 'quite perfect . . . the apotheosis of its type'. Its type is the traditional Scottish tower house, and its mellow stone, slender proportions and forthright decoration make Craigievar Castle one of the most attractive examples in Scotland. The castle's owner, Baron Sempill, agreed to sell on condition that it was given into the care of the National Trust for Scotland. £30,000 was raised for the purchase of the castle and thirty acres of land, and for the provision of facilities for visitors.

Craigievar is situated in rolling Grampian countryside, twenty-six miles west of Aberdeen and six miles from Alford. Its origins are closely linked with the fortunes of Aberdeen. In the fifteenth century the estate of Craigievar was owned by the Mortimer family, who were Aberdeen merchants. Early in the seventeenth century the Mortimers began the construction of a new house, but for some reason they were not able to carry on with it. In 1610 it was bought by William Forbes, who finished the building that became Craigievar Castle.

William Forbes, born in 1566, was the second son of the laird of Corse, not far away. Without the prospect of an inheritance he had to turn to another source of livelihood. He became a merchant, exporting through the port of Aberdeen goods such as salted salmon, woollens and hides, and importing mainly timber from Scandinavia and the Baltic. His commercial enterprise was acknowledged in his nickname, 'Danzig Willie'. In 1603 he married Margaret Woodward, the daughter of a provost of Edinburgh, and he and his wife began to buy estates in Forfarshire and Aberdeenshire. It was Craigievar that he decided to make his home.

It is not known to what extent he altered the original plans for the castle; what is certain is that the result is a captivating example of a style of building that is entirely Scottish, yet aware of ideas from elsewhere. It is alluring in itself, but its attractions are enhanced by the fact that it came at the end of a tradition, built at a time when the fortified house was almost an anachronism, and also by the fact that it has been virtually untouched since its first building. There were some nineteenth-century repairs and alterations, carried out in the 1820s by the Aberdeen architect John Smith, but these did not affect the traditional exterior. 'Danzig Willie' built a house with many defensive features - the single, unobtrusive entrance, the lack of windows at ground level — although the battlements at the top are ornamental rather than functional. The heart of the interior is the great hall, with its moulded plaster ceiling in a style so true to the Italian Renaissance that for a long time it was thought that the workmanship itself was Italian. It now seems likely that the work was carried out by English craftsmen, who may have been taught by Italians. The Trust has been careful to preserve these essential qualities, although this means controlling the number of visitors in certain parts of the castle at any one time. The plaster ceiling, in particular, is very vulnerable.

Craigievar is a splendid tribute to an old tradition. Due north is a Trust property that represents a modest response to new departures. The fortunes of the Leith family, who in 1650 built Leith Hall at Kennethmont, eight miles south of Huntly, were also tied up with Aberdeen. Although they owed their name to the port of Leith, where

*The Hall, Craigievar Castle, showing the plaster
ceiling.*

Part of the display of the military collection at Leith Hall.

Leith Hall.

The Music Room, one of the last additions to Leith Hall.

they were involved in shipping, by the middle of the fourteenth century they were with great success conducting the same business in Aberdeen. They did not confine their interests to Aberdeen itself, but bought land to the north and west, for land represented not only the security of ownership but revenue from the tenants who farmed it. Early in the seventeenth century James Leith and his wife Margaret Strachan of Glenkindie acquired land between the valleys of the Don and the Deveron rivers, and built a new house there. Leith Hall was given to the Trust in 1945 by the Hon Mrs Henrietta Leith-Hay, the house having remained with the family for nearly 300 years.

It was a modest four-storey white-harled house with corbelled turrets at each corner. In the eighteenth century extensions in a neo-classical style were added, but these still preserved some of the traditional vernacular detail of the original building. The Trust's work on Leith Hall has concentrated on maintaining its understated and friendly Georgian character, which aptly illustrates the role of the house and the family. Managing a house and land in a rural area more than thirty miles from Aberdeen was not easy. Even minimal subsistence farming was a struggle, and rural Aberdeenshire did not escape the ravages of the civil war that was still disrupting Scotland. The house's plain exterior was probably an apt indication of plain living within. The family's later history was a story of mixed fortunes, and the combined effects of growing prosperity and drastic upheaval which shaped the lives of so many in the eighteenth century. In moving away from a reliance on the sea this branch of the Leith family had linked their future more closely with a reliance on the land.

Overseas trade was the foundation of the prosperity of other maritime communities in Scotland, and their story underlines the importance of Scotland's independent contacts with the rest of Europe. Aberdeen, the unchallenged regional capital of the north-east, maintained her status and survived the union of the crowns, with its shift in commercial equilibrium to English centres and English controls. Other places fared less well, although their contribution was no less significant. The Trust has had an active involvement in a number of communities which illustrate this aspect of Scotland's history, and the first of these to claim the Trust's interest was Culross.

Culross played a crucial role in the earliest years of the Trust's history. In 1932, the year after the Trust's foundation, it acquired for £700 the Palace at Culross. The purchase price represented nearly half of the Trust's available funds at that time, but it was able to forge a partnership with the then HM Office of Works. The arrangement was that if the Trust bought the Palace the Office of Works would be responsible for repairs and refurbishment. The building is now in the guardianship of the Scottish Development Department, which has inherited this responsibility.

Culross Palace — not a 'palace' in the usual sense of the word, but a

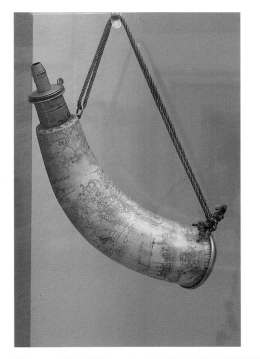

very fine town house — was built for Sir George Bruce in 1577. Sir George was the owner of Culross colliery, one of the factors contributing to the town's success. The origins of Culross go back to at least the sixth century, when it was an important religious centre. It is reputed to be the birthplace in 514 of St Mungo, the son of Princess Thenew of Lothian and patron saint of Glasgow. Legend tells that the princess incurred the wrath of her father, King Loth, through her relationship with a swineherd rather than the man of her father's choice. As punishment Loth had her cast adrift off Aberlady. But the boat was carried to Culross, where the monks of St Serf's monastery found her and her newborn son. The baby was called *Ceann Tichearn*, but was also known as *Munghu*, or 'Dearest Friend'. We are now more familiar with the names as Kentigern and Mungo. The ruins of the chapel built in 1503 to commemorate the princess's rescue still survive.

In 1217 a Cistercian Abbey was founded at Culross, and it was the monks who were first to mine the coal that was readily accessible on the shores of the Forth. In 1567 the Reformation caught up with the Abbey, which became the property of William Colville. It was Colville who brought in George Bruce to re-establish the colliery, which he did with such success that later he bought it. The coal was valuable for a number of industries that over the centuries grew up around the Forth, including pottery and glass-making, brewing and the manufacture of salt. The latter was particularly important, and a large proportion of Scotland's salt production was exported from the Firth of Forth salt pans.

The salt was manufactured by boiling seawater, and was thus dependent on cheap fuel. At Culross the fuel was on the doorstep, and it was on this close relationship between coal and salt that Sir George Bruce's success was founded. Sir George's career coincided with the zenith of the salt industry. Although Scottish salt was not of particularly good quality it was much in demand in the Baltic, Scandinavia and the Low Countries. It was a vital ingredient everywhere for the preservation of food, and particularly important for the fishing industry. By the seventeenth century cured fish were a major Scottish export, and by the end of the seventeenth century it was necessary to relax the Salt Laws, which favoured the salt producers, so that the fishing industry was paying less for its salt.

Another Culross industry closely linked with the availability of coal was the making of iron girdles for baking. Culross was famed for its baking girdles, which its smiths may in fact have invented. The story, like so many, brings us back to Robert the Bruce (of whom Sir George was a descendant), who withdrew his army to Culross in the summer of 1322, with Edward II at his heels. Bruce is said to have asked for iron plates so that his men could make oatcakes. There may be some truth in this as Bruce's scorched earth strategy, aimed at hindering the English, probably meant that his own army had little but oatmeal to eat.

MINERS, MARINERS AND MERCHANTS

The sixteenth-century activities of coal and salt masters such as Sir George Bruce contributed importantly to Scotland's identity as a trading nation. Culross itself was at this time a busy port, with sometimes as many as 170 foreign ships lying offshore waiting to pick up their cargoes. Many of the houses along the shores of the Forth and the Fife coast reflect the close contact with North Europe. On their return journey the ships that left the Forth with Scottish goods and materials often came back with red pantiles loaded as ballast, as well as timber, and ideas about how to use them. Pantile roofs are a feature of these coastal communities and buildings in other areas, including Edinburgh, often reveal in their architecture an influence from the Low Countries.

George Bruce vastly extended the workings of the mine dug by the monks, pushing them out for a mile under the Firth and digging 240 feet underground. The mine was visited by James VI, who was alarmed when he emerged from the shaft that opened out on Preston Island to find himself surrounded by water. It is remarkable that he entered the mine at all, for it must have been unpleasant and risky. The life of a coal miner was not only subject to the dangers and demands of the job itself. From 1606 there was a law which imposed virtual serfdom on colliers and salters, for they could not leave employment without obtaining release from their masters. This imposition in itself implies the hazards of the occupation. The effect of the law was to degrade not only the job but the collier's entire family, for by the end of the seventeenth century his wife and children were expected to join him in the mine, and they were all considered the property of the mine owner.

However, the full impact of this legislation came after the time of Sir George Bruce. His industrial achievement was marked by James VI, who in 1588 made Culross a royal burgh. It had been a burgh of barony, which meant more limited privileges than those of a royal burgh, since 1490. As a royal burgh Culross had more opportunities for trade and direct parliamentary representation, but it also contributed more revenue to the king. Sir George's new house was also a sign of his and the burgh's success.

The house is characteristic of the period, with crow-stepped gables, half-shuttered dormer windows with ornamental pediments and red pantiles, like most of the houses in Culross. During Bruce's lifetime the house was extended and improved, and a byre and stable block were added in 1611, the year in which he received his knighthood. Inside there are tempera-painted ceilings and painted wood-panelled walls. This decoration may have been part of the preparation for the visit of James VI in 1617. Sir George laid out a pleasant, terraced walled garden, which has now been reclaimed from its 1930s dereliction.

The Trust's purchase of Culross Palace was not only the first step in a continuing relationship with the community of Culross, it also heralded the evolution of an innovatory scheme for the preservation of some of

Scotland's more modest old dwellings. This initiative, the Little Houses Improvement Scheme, came about as a response to the need to rescue and preserve properties under threat from developers or simply in very bad state of repair. Attention was focused on the need in the 1930s, when slum clearance policy took a rather indiscriminatory view of dilapidated housing, and was sweeping away buildings of real interest and importance. Initial action in Edinburgh resulted in the Trust setting up an Old Edinburgh Committee to list and assess the city's old buildings. With the generous provision of funds by the fourth Marquess of Bute it became possible to extend this into a national survey, which looked at a hundred towns in Scotland and listed well over a thousand traditional buildings, identifying 136 of these as outstanding.

Although the Second World War interrupted progress, a momentum of interest and action led to co-operative efforts to preserve a number of buildings. The objective was to make buildings habitable, either restored to their original function or adapted to something new. The Town and Country Planning (Scotland) Act of 1947 required that a list of buildings of 'special architectural or historical interest' be prepared, which made destruction more difficult, if not impossible. The Trust provided positive demonstration of what could be achieved in terms of preservation and rehabilitation.

In some ways it was a fortuitous blending of the pragmatic involvement that had been part of the Trust's strategy from the earliest years with a more broadly-based concern for conservation. Those initial steps in Culross were vital. There followed major involvement in Dunkeld and on the Fife Coast. Efforts were given a new lease of life in 1960, with the creation of a Revolving Fund, which was based on the purchase, restoration and reselling of endangered properties. The buildings were resold with a conservation agreement that committed the new owners to make no change to use or design without the consent of the Trust. The initial capital to set this going came from the Pilgrim Trust and the General Fund of the National Trust for Scotland. This amounted to the sum of £20,000, which seems modest now; in fact the beginnings of the scheme were much more modest, with the few hundred pounds spent in Culross in the 1930s.

The scheme has proved itself to be both purposeful and flexible, and within its framework have operated varied and co-operative solutions to the rescue of buildings under threat. By mid-1990 162 houses had been restored under the scheme, in addition to the thirty-nine houses in Culross and twenty-three in Dunkeld that were worked on before the Little Houses Improvement Scheme had begun. Its operation and achievement have generated considerable interest in Europe, where a number of countries have followed the Trust's pioneering lead. In 1976 the European prize for the restoration of historic monuments was awarded by the FVS Foundation of Hamburg to the Trust with special

The Study, Culross, before restoration (left) and after (right).

The Ell Shop, Dunkeld, before restoration (left) and after.

Cathedral Street, Dunkeld, before restoration (left) and after (right).

reference to the scheme's achievement. The award brought a sum of money which was invested as a fund for travel in Europe. One of the beneficiaries of this was The Hill House, designed by Charles Rennie Mackintosh, which came to the Trust in 1982. The fund enabled a member of the Trust's staff to make a research visit abroad to work on Mackintosh.

In Culross the Trust not only purchased the Palace, but also acquired, before the beginning of the War, twenty other properties, all desperately in need of rescue. Amongst these were the Study, dating from the early seventeenth century, with its distinctive corbelled Outlook Tower. It was the tower that was used as a study, so tradition has it, by Bishop Leighton of Dunblane when he visited Culross. Inside there are panelled walls and a fine painted ceiling.

Other Trust houses in Culross reflect the occupation pursued in the town. Coal mining and salt panning dwindled, and gradually the burgh's merchant activities also declined. But seamen still lived in Culross, and Tanhouse, Snuff Cottage, the Coachman's Cottage and the Butcher's House are reminders of the needs and activities of the community. Bessie Bar's Hall was the malthouse of Elizabeth Paterson, active in the late sixteenth and early seventeenth centuries. Another characteristic Culross exterior tactfully disguises an electricity sub-station. In 1975 Culross Town Council gave the seventeenth-century Townhouse with the original Council Chambers and Tolbooth to the Trust, and it now houses a Tourist Information Centre on the ground floor.

Up the hill are the parish church, rebuilt in 1633, and the remains of the Abbey. Inside the church is a monument to Sir George Bruce, his wife and their eight children, while in the churchyard tombstones tell their tale of the life and work of Culross. Nearby, Culross Abbey House was built in 1608 for Edward Bruce, Sir George's brother, who became Lord Kinross. It was for the early seventeenth century a very modern design, and contrasts strikingly with its more traditional neighbours. In the nineteenth century the house was lived in by Admiral Thomas Cochrane, tenth Earl of Dundonald. Admiral Cochrane is remembered best for his contribution to the struggles for independence in South America and Greece. His father Archibald, the ninth Earl, was one of the more advanced colliery owners in the area, and made significant contributions to industrial chemistry.

Many of Scotland's burghs experienced growth and prosperity in the sixteenth and seventeenth centuries. Scottish merchants were not as venturesome as some of their European counterparts, who were gaining footholds in the east and the New World, but they were confident and canny, and ready to spend many years abroad in the interests of trade. Scots became well known in a number of North European cities, Rotterdam, for example, and Stockholm, Warsaw, Danzig and London. In their absence it was very often their wives who ran the home base of the business. Culross itself had close contacts with Veere, the Scottish staple or market for imports in the Netherlands, where Scots merchants enjoyed corporate privileges, and where the Scottish factor's house is now preserved. This link was celebrated in 1981, the Trust's Golden Jubilee Year, with the twinning of Culross and Veere and an exchange of visits by sea. A privileged relationship also existed with Bordeaux which accounted for the large quantities of claret that were imported into Scotland. Sometimes Scots who went abroad never returned, finding they could readily and productively settle in their adopted country, often making a significant contribution.

Characteristic was the fact that the success of Scottish trade was not confined to the larger ports. Many smaller places on the Forth and the east coast burgeoned. Bo'ness, for example, across the Forth from Culross, and also a mining and salt-panning town, grew rapidly at this time. Along the Fife coast the small fishing communities and trading ports were becoming more substantial. There was money to build in stone, in place of vulnerable timber, and the Trust has had a hand in preserving a number of these early stone buildings. At Pittenweem, for example, which became a royal burgh in 1542 in recognition of its trading activity and potential, a number of houses were the direct result of commercial success. These include Gyles House, a seventeenth-century sea-captain's home, and the Gyles next door, a slightly later building. Kellie Lodging was built in 1590 as a town house for the Oliphant family, the same Oliphants who built Kellie Castle three miles inland. The fact that the Oliphants felt the need for a house in Pittenweem was itself a mark of the port's status. Kellie Lodging was restored by the Trust in 1972.

The Trust has also been active in nearby St Monans, a fishing port from the time of the fourteenth century, where eighteenth- and nineteenth-century houses have been restored. In Dysart, close to Kirkcaldy, the Trust collaborated with Kirkcaldy Town Council in a major programme of restoration and building. Among the houses concerned are the Anchorage, the Pilot's House, the Shoremaster's House and the Tide-Waiter's House, all evidence of Dysart's history as a port. Also preserved is the home of John McDouall Stuart, the nineteenth-century explorer of Australia. Further north, several buildings in Crail and Anstruther have benefited from the rehabilitation programme — indeed, Crail saw the first of the restorations under the Revolving Fund. Both these fishing communities also have their origins in the Middle Ages, and their histories echo those of other coastal villages.

It was not only the ports that flourished as a result of the commercial activity of the sixteenth and seventeenth centuries. Inland burghs also benefited. Linlithgow is a good example of a town that achieved its commercial heyday at this time. Linlithgow was one of the larger centres of trade. It had been a royal burgh since 1388, and benefited from the interest in Linlithgow Palace as a royal residence. There was a number of craft guilds in the town, which became particularly noted for its tanneries. Its overseas trade was conducted through its port at Blackness on the Forth, one of Scotland's busiest ports in the sixteenth century. The royal household was a vigorous stimulus to trade, which brought in luxury goods from abroad for the Palace.

Two houses in Linlithgow's High Street were restored by the Trust in 1958. Their late sixteenth-century date is signified by the fact that their gable-ends face onto the street, a characteristic feature of burgh town planning at that time. Linlithgow, like other towns at that time, was rebuilding itself in stone, and the Trust's houses are probably the oldest surviving examples of this period of renewal. The houses are associated with the Hamiltons, a prominent local family with an estate at Pardovan, three miles from the town. In the last six years the Trust has continued its work on small houses with a number of innovatory projects, including the Dutch Gable House, Greenock, Dunbar's Hospital, Church Street, Inverness, the Old Granary at the City Mills, Perth and 5 Charlotte Street, Glasgow designed by Robert Adam. The policy has been to focus on key buildings, whose rehabilitation enhances the original atmosphere of the area.

The centre of Scotland's trade remained Edinburgh. Although the departure of James VI to London had shifted the court and much of its connected culture and business, the Scottish Parliament stayed in Edinburgh and life in the city expressed commercial, professional and religious energy. Presbyterianism had taken root, although it would remain an issue of debate and conflict for most of the century. Religious riots were not uncommon on the streets of Edinburgh, especially after the attempt of Charles I to impose a new service book on the Scottish church. The citizens of Edinburgh on the whole supported the National Covenant of 1638, which consolidated resistance to what was seen as a threat to property and religion from Charles's arbitrary kingship.

The thriving, congested city was still building. Its thirty thousand or so inhabitants were packed into a small space limited by topography and the need for protection. The High Street, described by one late sixteenth-century visitor as a 'broad and very fair street', joining the Castle on its rock with Holyrood Palace 'over which a high mountain hangs', defined the scope and scale of the city. Off the High Street a herring-bone pattern of wynds and closes was stacked high with tenements or lands which cut out the light and intensified the filth and the stench. Middens were piled in the street, and the Town Council's attempts to have them removed were inadequate. Although it is unlikely that any seventeenth-century city was particularly sweet smelling, Edinburgh attracted particular comment in that respect. 'I never came to my lodgings in Edinburgh', said one seventeenth-century traveller, 'or went out, but I was constrained to hold my nose.' Unlike most other contemporary cities Edinburgh was not built on a river, which could

Gladstone's Land, Lawnmarket, Edinburgh.

The painted Chamber in Gladstone's Land (overleaf).

serve, like London's Thames, as a city's sewer.

Yet it was a fine city, and bent on improvement. The 1630s saw the building of Parliament House and of the Tron Kirk. Heriot's Hospital was built, with an endowment from 'Jingling Geordie' Heriot, who had made his fortune as a goldsmith and money-lender to the king. And it was not just building on a grand scale that was changing the High Street. The old timber-fronted, thatched houses, a fire risk and a hindrance, were being restructured with stone. Although the tall, multi-storeyed houses were still crammed with people attempts were made to create space inside of some grace if not of grandeur. Later in the century came a water supply piped in from Comiston — though water still had to be fetched from one of the street wells and often carried up several flights of stairs (Defoe, in Edinburgh early in the eighteenth century, commented on the 'Scarcity of Water') — and other facilities, such as the

more organized provision of markets.

Gladstone's Land, the Trust's house in the Lawnmarket, is a splendid illustration of this period in Edinburgh's history. The house was built in December 1617 by Thomas Gledstanes and his wife Bessie Cunningham, and it was probably at that time, like most of the High Street houses, a stone and timber structure with a front about twenty-three feet back from its present line. The ground floor would have been an arcade which sheltered booths. Virtually the whole of the High Street was in effect a market place, with business of all kinds carried on in the streets and in the taverns. There was little space for separate business premises.

Thomas Gledstanes was a merchant, and in 1610 had been admitted Burgess of Edinburgh, a position which gave him both commercial privileges and political power. Edinburgh merchants traded through Leith, and Customs Books for Leith show him trading in prunes, iron, pots, honey and vinegar. Merchants at that time did not specialize, but put their money into any venture or cargo that looked promising, often joining with others to share the risk, which could be great. In 1627 Gledstanes lost a cargo to Dunkirk pirates, and in the years that followed seemed to be under financial pressure, borrowing money in 1628 and selling part of his land in 1631.

But by that time he had transformed his home. The entire front of the house was built out in stone, to allow new large rooms on each of the main storeys: the original front of the building can still be seen. The Trust's restoration of the house has entailed removing later alterations and reinstating features such as the half-shuttered windows. This has involved a considerable amount of careful reconstruction, and reproduction of features such as chandeliers, sconces and cruisie lamps, much of which has been carried out in the Trust's own workshop to designs based on suitable originals. The *gled* or hawk seems to have been adopted by Thomas Gledstanes as an emblem of his name, and the hanging sign and gilded *gled* on the outside of the building were also made in the Trust's workshop.

Restoration has been extensive and in two phases. The house came to the Trust in 1934, a gift from Helen Harrison, a social worker who had got to know the house through her work in what was at that time one of Edinburgh's slum areas. The house was originally restored by Sir Frank Mears, and then leased to the Saltire Society, who occupied it until 1978. It was then decided to return the house as nearly as possible to its seventeenth-century character and open it to the public. The combined efforts of Robert Hurd and Partners, Trust staff and Stenhouse Conservation Centre achieved striking results.

Two of Gladstone's Land's most interesting features were discovered in 1934. These were the arcaded ground floor, which had long since disappeared behind shop fronts, and the painted ceiling on the second floor. Thomas Gledstanes had the ceiling of his fine new room painted in the style that had become popular throughout Scotland. The paintwork survived under layers of later paint and plaster. The decorated frieze on the wall also contributed to the impression of status and success which the house as a whole conveys. The original function of the ground floor is recaptured in the Trust's reconstruction of a cloth merchant's booth which shows samples of cloth as well as a cutting table and an ell measure — the ell, thirty-seven inches, was the standard measure of the time.

In the rest of the house the furnishing is seventeenth century, except in the 'Green Room'. Its eighteenth-century panelling suggested refurbishment in similar style, and this has been carried out with furnishings dating mainly from the early part of the century. It represents the end of an era for Edinburgh's High Street, for the old town was overflowing to the point when space for expansion had to be found. Eyes were looking north to the area beyond the Nor' Loch at the foot of the castle crag. In 1767 James Craig's plans for a new town were adopted. By the end of the century the exodus from the old town to the newly laid-out squares and streets below was well under way.

Thomas and Bessie Gledstanes would never have occupied the whole of the house that came to be known as Gledstane's Land. Tenement living traditionally set families on top of one another, with tradesmen and craftsmen occupying the ground level, nearest to the dirt and smells of the street, and the poorest in the attic floors, furthest from the water. The wealthier residents were usually found in the middle storeys, and these could include merchants, lawyers and members of the aristocracy. This cheek-by-jowl living changed totally when those who could afford to moved into the spacious New Town.

CHAPTER FIVE

Risings and Resistance

FROM the time of the Covenanters' first resistance, from 1637, Scotland was crisscrossed by war for over a hundred years. There were few, if any, corners of the country that were not affected in some way, and most of the Trust's properties that were then in existence were touched by these religious and political struggles.

Most quarrels in Scotland sooner or later involved England. Although the two kingdoms were united, and from 1707 the two parliaments, war was still a major factor in Scotland's history, and the two Bishops' Wars against Charles I saw successful Scottish invasions of England in 1639-40. Andrew, Lord Fraser, supported the Covenant, as did many in the Aberdeen area, and entertained James Graham, Earl of Montrose, prominent amongst the Covenanting leaders, at Castle Fraser. Lord Fraser was involved in the fighting at Towie Barclay Castle and Turriff, and participated in an attack on Aberdeen. Reprisal came when Royalist troops laid siege to the castle. Although the castle itself remained unscathed the surrounding policies were burned.

Montrose returned to Aberdeen in 1644, but now he was at the head of Royalist troops. He found he could not in good conscience accept the constitutional implications of the Covenant, and so had returned his allegiance to Charles. This time the attack on Aberdeen was particularly bloody; Montrose was unable to control his troops, especially a force of MacDonalds from Ulster. And the lands of Lord Fraser did not escape, for Montrose burned his 'ritche corne yairdes' and 'spoilzeit his ground'.

On his way north Montrose had camped outside Crathes. Sir Thomas Burnett, though sympathetic to the Covenanting cause, did not take up arms. Montrose was an old friend, and he entertained him to dinner. The result was a letter granting immunity to Crathes for the duration of the wars, something which had already been granted by the Covenanters. The two letters still survive.

Drum Castle was less lucky. The Irvines were Royalists, and Alexander, the tenth laird, was Sheriff of Aberdeen when Montrose made his first visit. He escaped from the town as the Covenanting troops marched in. Later, when he was away fighting, the castle was besieged by the troops of General Monroe. Lady Irvine surrendered, and the castle was occupied and plundered. The estate was ransacked to feed the troops, not the least of the ways in which the land suffered in time of war. Drum was occupied three times more and the castle and its lands plundered before the Civil War came to an end. Members of the family suffered exile and imprisonment. In 1644 the Marquess of Argyll evicted Lady Irvine, his own niece, and her mother-in-law, allowing them to take virtually nothing with them, before ransacking the castle.

At Craigievar Sir William Forbes was a fervent Covenanter who fought against Montrose at Aberdeen in 1644. Although he was captured during the battle Craigievar itself was safe — indeed, Sir William transported goods there from his more vulnerable Aberdeenshire lands. As troops moved back and forth across Aberdeenshire for a dozen or so years the Forbes and other landowning families were probably thankful for homes that did not compromise the need for defence. For all Craigievar's elegance the windowless ground floor still had a purpose.

Further north at Brodie House near Forres (it did not become Brodie Castle until the nineteenth century) Alexander Brodie was a zealous Presbyterian and signed the National Covenant in 1638. In 1645 Brodie was attacked by Lord Lewis Gordon at the instigation of Montrose, but though fired and plundered the house survived. After the execution of Charles I, which shook Scottish opinion, Brodie was at The Hague as part of the deputation sent to the exiled Charles II. Charles landed at Garmouth on the Moray Firth in 1651, where he was persuaded to sign the Solemn League and Covenant, which pledged him to retaining the Presbyterian church. He then proceeded to Scone for his coronation which Brodie attended. The Brodie line continued his religious and political convictions. Alexander, nineteenth Brodie of Brodie, was a staunch Whig, an MP for more than thirty years, and did service in the army of the Duke of Cumberland against the Jacobites. In his absence his wife Mary Sleigh Brodie looked after Cumberland's troops — Brodie House was not far from the battlefield at Culloden.

The house that Lord Lewis Gordon attacked in 1645 was relatively new, having been built in 1567 by Alexander Brodie as a Z-plan tower house. There were some changes to the house in the eighteenth century, and especially to the grounds, but no major development until the nineteenth, when the house was enlarged.

Brodie Castle, with its contents and 125 acres of land, came into the care of the Trust in 1980, through the National Land Fund. Ninian Brodie of Brodie provided an endowment, which enabled the Trust to undertake the rehabilitation necessary before the castle could be opened to the public. Ninian Brodie's continued participation in the life and interpretation of the castle is an essential feature of its character. He lives in a wing of the castle and acts as a welcoming and incomparably informative guide to visitors. This kind of partnership, which is found in other Trust properties, for example the House of the Binns, is characteristic of the Trust's flexible *modus operandi*.

Covenanting resistance merged into Civil War. The Covenanters initially supported the English Parliament, and in 1643 the Covenanting army joined the English Parliamentary forces. But the execution of Charles I in 1649 put an end to that alliance, for it was

Restoration work in progress in the Drawing Room at Brodie Castle.

The Drawing Room at Brodie Castle, restoration complete.

beyond what the Covenanters could accept. In 1650 Cromwell came north, and defeated a Covenanting army at Dunbar before entering Edinburgh. By this time Montrose, who had been waging a guerrilla war in the Highlands, had been captured and executed.

The name of Graham did not die. John Graham of Claverhouse, the nephew of James Graham of Montrose, was two years old when his uncle was executed, but would grow up to take part in the final, and in some ways most savage, chapter of the Covenanting story. He was in command of the forces used to suppress the Covenanters in the south-west after their defeat by General Tam Dalyell at Rullion Green in the Pentlands. (General Dalyell's family home was the House of the Binns.) Graham's success during the 'Killing Times' earned him the nickname 'Bluidy Clavers' and the title of Viscount Dundee. But another change in political and religious direction made 'Bonnie Dundee' the enemy of the government.

Viscount Dundee became the first Jacobite leader, supporting James VII who was deposed in 1688 in favour of William of Orange and his wife Mary, James's daughter. In the summer of 1689 Scotland was as divided as ever. The situation was potentially explosive, with a new government run by the Estates or Scots parliament on behalf of King William and many in the Highlands ready to follow James VII. It was this support for James that Dundee attempted to rally. During that summer he moved into the Highlands, having raised the standard of the exiled king on Dundee Law. But although some Highland leaders joined him neither his charm nor his proven courage could persuade the clans into a large scale uprising. After some initial success he had to face government forces commanded by General Mackay, a seasoned and canny campaigner.

Their encounter took place on terrain eminently unsuitable for pitched battle, near the narrow, craggy Pass of Killiecrankie. General Mackay was at a disadvantage, with Dundee's Highland troops on the hillside above him. Although Mackay's troops were better equipped, with modern firearms, and subject to professional discipline, they could not withstand a Highland charge with broadswords. With his troops severely mauled by this ferocious charge Mackay was able to rally only 400 of his original 4000 men and lead them in retreat to Aberfeldy. For the Royalists the battle was won but the cause lost, although it would revive. Dundee, like hundreds of his Highlanders, had been hit by a musket shot. He died the next day. Without his leadership the Highland Army, after making an attempt to take Dunkeld, returned to the hills. The following year what remained of the army was routed by Mackay's cavalry at Cromdale in Speyside.

The fifty-four acres of the Pass of Killiecrankie held by the Trust do not include the actual battleground, which remains in private hands. But they are both dramatic in themselves and evoke the drama and terror of the battle's aftermath. It is also a reminder of the main route north, connecting Perth and Inverness. Though hardly a road — Mackay's soldiers made their way in single file, or at most two abreast — until General Wade built one forty years later, it was both a lifeline and a route for marching armies. The crags, the steep slopes and the foaming river were all reminders to those going north that they were entering wild country.

The interpretation of battlefields is often difficult, sometimes

The River Garry at Killiecrankie.

because the landscape has changed significantly, but often because such demands are required of the imagination to recreate the sights and sounds of battle. The Trust early on recognized the need to provide information for the public at its battlefield sites. The original Visitor Centre at Killiecrankie was the result of a pioneering approach in the 1950s to roadside interpretation, inspired partly by the visit of Trust staff to some of the American national parks. The interpretation of the Killiecrankie site now provides the background material necessary to understand the battle and its significance, and also highlights features of environmental interest. In the Pass itself a particular attraction is the 'Soldier's Leap', the point where Duncan MacBean, one of Mackay's soldiers, is said to have leapt across the River Garry. Fear of the pursuing Highlanders must have lent wings to his heels, for he cleared eighteen feet. Many of his comrades were less lucky, and drowned as they attempted to escape the dirks and broadswords.

The Jacobite attack on Dunkeld was in a sense an afterthought, but the results were devastating. It was garrisoned by a single regiment, the Cameronians, who had gained their name from the passionate fighting preacher Richard Cameron. When the Highlanders moved in and occupied some of the houses, the Cameronians locked the doors and fired them. There ensued appalling slaughter, and the destruction by fire of most of the town. Only the cathedral and three houses survived.

It was some years before there was effective rebuilding in Dunkeld,

Looking down Glencoe from Aonach Eagach.

and it is some of those houses built in the eighteenth-century reconstruction that have been the beneficiaries of the Trust's commitment
to rescue. The town centre retains the character of an early eighteenth-
century small burgh, with many vernacular features yet with a flavour of
neo-classical proportions. The Trust owns twenty houses in the High
Street and Cathedral Street, all privately occupied and so not open to
the public, but evidence of the successful collaborative restoration
undertaken between 1954 and 1965 by the Trust and the County
Council. The Trust's shop, the Ell Shop, so named after the weaver's
measure embedded in the wall, is evidence of one of the occupations
that sustained Dunkeld in the eighteenth century before handweaving
was ousted by machines.

Highland resistance to William III continued, although for the rest
of the century it was negative rather than active. It was a reluctance to
take the oath of allegiance to the king that was partly responsible for the
Glencoe massacre, an event that has inevitably stamped a particular
resonance on the place and the word. The historical significance of the
area is an important part of the Trust's responsibility in their care of
Glencoe. It begins centuries before the bloody events of February 1692.
Glencoe's associations with Fingal, the great Celtic hero, whom history
links with the third century AD and myth with battles against both the
Romans and the Vikings, are enhanced by the brooding nature of the
landscape. Fingal's Scottish persona owes much to the reconstructions
of the eighteenth-century poetry of James Macpherson, but in Glencoe
one can understand something of Macpherson's inspiration.

According to legend the battle with the Vikings, led by King Erragon,
took place near Ballachulish on the shores of Loch Leven. It culminated
in a series of contests between 140 warriors on each side. Erragon was
eventually defeated, and only two of the original forty Viking ships
escaped down Loch Leven. Eleven grave slabs at West Laroch are
popularly associated with the Vikings. Fingal may have been victorious,
but later Glencoe was in the hands of a clan of Viking descent, the
MacDougalls. Their position, based at Dunstaffnage Castle, was
destroyed when they fought against Robert the Bruce, unlike the
Macdonalds, whose chief, Angus Og, played a vital role in Bruce's
ultimate success. Angus Og was rewarded with the gift of Glencoe, and
it remained Macdonald country.

A recurring feature of Highland history is the rivalry between the
Macdonalds and the Campbells. Although they both supported Bruce,
over subsequent centuries they raided each other relentlessly. Much
blood was shed, in Glencoe and elsewhere, before the episode that is
remembered as a massacre, and the tradition of clan hostility played a
part, though a minor one, in the events. The massacre was the result of a
plot organized on orders from London by a secretary of state with no
clan loyalties himself.

The Campbells supported King William and Protestantism.

William inherited the problem that had troubled every ruler of the kingdom, on its own or with England, that of controlling the Highland clans. William had little interest in Scotland but wanted to remove the possibility of disorder as quickly as possible. The Master of Stair, Secretary of State for Scotland, singled out the Glencoe Macdonalds for the purpose of making an example. There was a reluctance amongst some chiefs to take the oath of allegiance to William, which was required by 1 January 1692. Eventually MacIain of the Macdonalds, a few days late, travelled to Inveraray, the heart of Campbell territory, to do so. But Stair had no intention of reversing his orders. On 1 February two companies of government troops under the command of Captain Robert Campbell of Glenlyon set off from Fort William for Glencoe. Everyone, including the Glencoe people, thought they were on their way to attack MacDonnel of Glengarry, whose Jacobite sympathies were well known.

At Glencoe Captain Campbell and his men received the hospitality of the Macdonalds. Traditions of enmity came second to traditions of hospitality. For ten days the troops were entertained. On 12 February Captain Campbell received orders from Fort William to kill all Macdonalds under the age of seventy. Early the next day, on a bitterly cold wintry morning, the slaughter commenced. Although the murderous breach of hospitality was a terrible offence to Highland tradition, the massacre was not as effective as intended. The homes of the Macdonalds were scattered over a wide area, and the bad weather favoured those who knew the terrain. Contrary to orders, the troops had failed to seal the passes. The chief himself was killed, but his two sons and grandson escaped, along with about three hundred others. The 120 government soldiers managed to kill about thirty-eight members of the Macdonald clan. The sense of outrage and betrayal was all the greater for the fact that Captain Campbell's niece was married to the Macdonald chief's younger son.

Although there were Campbells among the troops the massacre was the result of government strategy rather than an episode in clan warfare, even if the manner of execution built on ancient hostilities. The political repercussions of the massacre were considerable. Sir John Dalrymple, Master of Stair, had chosen the target for a punitive strike, but had underestimated public reaction. When the facts of the massacre came to light public opinion was horrified, and the Scots parliament condemned Stair, who resigned his post as Secretary of State but was protected from punishment by William.

In spite of the political scandal the pacification appeared to be successful. But in 1715 Alastair Macdonald of Glencoe, brother of the chief, fought for the Jacobite cause. Also fighting for the man whom the Jacobites thought of as James VIII was another John, the son of Captain Robert Campbell. The fourteenth Chief, another Alastair, came out for Charles Edward Stewart in 1745, and was a member of the Prince's council. After Culloden the Glencoe Macdonalds suffered again. The new house built by John the thirteenth Chief was destroyed and Glencoe was devastated by retributive burning and plunder. Its emptiness, which for the twentieth-century visitor is part of its appeal, is a relatively recent phenomenon. But it is not empty of historical reverberations, and the best supplement to the information available at the Trust's Visitor Centre is an investigation on foot of the glen itself. This might include a walk to Signal Rock, where, it is reputed, the signal was given for the killing to commence.

The quelling of Highland resistance to a Protestant and, as considered by the Jacobites, unrightful monarch was temporary. James VII died in 1700, but his son, another James, was regarded by many as king. In 1708 a French fleet with James Edward Stewart and over 5000 men on board approached the Firth of Forth, but twenty-eight men-of-war and a storm sent them back to France. It was a missed opportunity, as a year after the union of the parliaments and with the disaster of the Scottish expedition to Darien still fresh in the memory, there was strong anti-English feeling. Seven years later the Jacobite standard was raised on the Braes of Mar, and a number of the clans joined the army mustered by the Earl of Mar in the name of James VIII.

Amongst those who followed Mar was Charles, Lord Fraser, in spite of his family's Covenanting past. Mar was an indecisive leader, and slow to take advantage of what could have been favourable circumstances. A battle was fought against government troops at Sheriffmuir: neither side could claim a victory. The Jacobites needed a conclusive result and firm action to hold their enterprises together. Neither was forthcoming. When James arrived in Scotland at the end of the year the rising had already failed. Lord Fraser, on the run after the debacle, fell to his death from cliffs near the fishing village of Pennan. He was succeeded by his stepson – he had married a widow, Lady Marjorie Erskine whose first husband had been Simon Fraser of Inverallochy – whose grandson, another Charles, fought at Culloden.

The Laird of Drum, the fourteenth, also fought at Sheriffmuir, where he received a wound in the head. He died insane a few years later, and the estate of Drum, sadly depleted by decades of war, passed to his uncle, John Irvine. The Irvines' Jacobite convictions remained undeterred by the sufferings of Drum. John Irvine's son Alexander fought at Culloden, and was in hiding afterwards in a secret room in Drum Castle. The cool action of his sister, who misdirected the pursuing troops, saved him from capture but not from exile.

On the other side of the country, Kintail, now in the care of the Trust, lost many men in the Battle of Sheriffmuir. Four years later the area would suffer again. A second Jacobite expedition sailed from Spain. Only two of the ships reached Scotland, and sailed up Loch Alsh and Loch Duich to Kintail. The few hundred troops, led by the Earl Marischal, a veteran of the Fifteen, camped by Eilean Donan castle. But

Glenfinnan and the Monument to the Jacobite Rising of 1745.

although they were joined by a handful of clansmen there was little support, and the remaining ships never arrived. Royal Navy warships followed them up Loch Duich, bombarded the castle and destroyed the kirk at Kintail and several of the surrounding homesteads. At Glen Shiel the small band of invaders was attacked and defeated by government troops. It was a minor episode in the story of Jacobite resistance, and it did nothing to change the convictions of the people of Kintail, who remained loyal to the Stewarts.

Prince Charles Edward Stewart landed near Arisaig in July 1745 and raised his standard at Glenfinnan at the head of Loch Shiel, where he was joined by some of the clans who had long been preparing for his coming. In 1938 the monument built by Alexander Macdonald of Glenaladale to commemorate the event was given to the Trust, and the following year Archibald MacKellaig entered into a restrictive agreement with the Trust to ensure the care of twenty-eight acres of surrounding land. The first Visitor Centre at Glenfinnan was opened in 1966. Generous grants enabled the Trust to redevelop the Centre and improve the information facilities for visitors. The new Visitor Centre was opened in summer 1983. Each summer sees the holding of the Glenfinnan Games, supported by the Trust, with the enthusiastic involvement of the surrounding communities.

The story of the Forty Five has been coloured by much emotion and mythology, and the landscape itself has played a role in sustaining its

The annual Glenfinnan Games.

romantic appeal. James Edward Stewart never returned to Scotland after the failure of the Fifteen. He had been a young man of twenty-seven then; now his son, at twenty-five, proclaimed his father king. But the intervening thirty years had seen much activity in the Highlands, designed to make control, and if necessary pacification, of the clans more effective. There were now well-constructed roads where there had once been paths or tracks, bridges where there had been only fords. Fort Augustus was built, and Fort William and Fort George (on its original site at Inverness) strengthened. In addition, many of the clans had adjusted to the changes brought about by the Union and a new royal family, the Hanoverians. Prince Charles was disappointed at the small numbers that gathered at Glenfinnan or joined him on his march south, though he found the new military roads a great help.

He met with initial success, and a victory at Prestonpans encouraged him to continue south, across the Border. There was little support from the English and he was forced to retreat. The dispirited army returned to Glasgow, reached on Christmas Day, and then on towards Inverness. The Prince spent seven weeks at Inverness. It was difficult to keep his army together. Many had drifted away in the course of retreat; the need to forage and the wish simply to return home dispersed others.

Meanwhile an army under the Duke of Cumberland, second son of George II, drew nearer. Cumberland was shortly to celebrate his twenty-fifth birthday, the same age as Charles Edward when he landed

The raising of the standard at Glenfinnan.
(W. Skeach-Cumming, courtesy of the
National Galleries of Scotland).

Culloden: the battlefield.

Re-thatching Old Leanach Cottage, Culloden.

in Scotland. By the end of February 1746 Cumberland and his troops were in Aberdeen. Six weeks later they were camped at Nairn. Prince Charles gathered what was left of his army and left Inverness, his first intention to launch a night attack on Cumberland. When that plan was abandoned he drew up a battle line on Drumossie Moor, about a mile from Culloden House, between Inverness and Nairn.

Every circumstance was against a Jacobite victory. The Prince's army was by this time less than 5000 strong. The Duke of Cumberland had 9000 men, backed by naval ships in the Moray Firth. The ground chosen for the battle, a flat and empty moor, favoured the Duke's artillery, the manoeuvring and musket fire of well-drilled infantry and the impetus of the cavalry charge. It was the choice of the Prince's Irish adjutant O'Sullivan, and his more experienced and more astute commander Lord George Murray had serious misgivings. 'Not one

single souldier but would have been against such a ffeeld had their advice been askt', he wrote later. It was not 'proper for Highlanders', who fought their best charging over rough terrain that was a hindrance to regular troops.

The Jacobite army was disadvantaged in other ways. The prospect of a night attack on Cumberland's troops at Nairn was tempting: they were celebrating the Duke's birthday and were likely to be, as Lord George put it, 'as drunk as beggars'. The Jacobites marched all night, to realize as they neared their destination that daylight was only an hour away and that to continue with their plans would be suicidal. The men had begun the march cold and hungry, for supplies had been left at Inverness. By the time they had returned to Culloden they were also exhausted. Many flung themselves on the ground to sleep, and did not wake in time for the ensuing battle. Some did not wake at all.

The clansmen drawn up to face the Duke of Cumberland included Camerons, Stewarts of Appin, Clan Chattan, Frasers, Chisholms, Macdonalds, MacGregors, Farquharsons, MacLaughlans, MacLeans, MacLeods and Mackenzies, and smaller groups from a number of other clans. They were mostly on foot, ill-equipped, ill-protected from the wind and sleet, tired and hungry. There were also some French and Irish troops, and cavalry, though there were few horses.

Cumberland's men approached from Nairn and briskly formed their battle line. The battle began with a lengthy cannonade from Cumberland's artillery, which did great damage but did not break the Jacobite ranks. The Highland troops were accustomed to the charge and hand to hand fighting. They stood firm but grew angry and impatient as the artillery continued its deadly effects and there was no order to charge. When at last the order came their ranks had been drastically thinned, and they encountered musket fire and bayonets.

The battle was lost and won in less than an hour. Prince Charles was led from the field. He had witnessed devastating slaughter but was spared the sight of the carnage that would follow, when the Duke of Cumberland's army systematically and ruthlessly carried out appalling reprisals. Some of Cumberland's own men were disgusted by the cold-blooded butchery. Many instances of individual heroism are recorded, not least those surrounding the protection and eventual escape from Scotland of the hunted Charles Edward. It is estimated that about a thousand died on the battlefield. Many more were executed later, either on the spot when they were discovered, or after arrest and trial.

No other name in Scottish history has quite the resonance of Culloden, and the place itself has been a major focus of Trust activity since it first became involved with Culloden in 1937. Culloden Moor was still imbued with an atmosphere of loss and loneliness, which the memorial cairn and worn markers of the graves of the clans put up in 1881 by the tenth laird of Culloden, Duncan Forbes, only enhanced. Agriculture had to some extent changed the face of the battlefield, and a

THE BATTLE
OF CULLODEN
WAS FOUGHT ON THIS MOOR
16TH APRIL 1746.

THE GRAVES OF THE
GALLANT HIGHLANDERS
WHO FOUGHT FOR
SCOTLAND & PRINCE CHARLIE,
ARE MARKED BY THE NAMES
OF THEIR CLANS.

The inscription on the Memorial Cairn erected by Duncan Forbes at Culloden in 1881.

road ran through it, but without destroying its bleak aura. The 1937 gift of land by Alexander Munro of Leanach Farm was added to in 1944 by Hector Forbes of Culloden, when he gave to the Trust the area with the graves and the memorial, Old Leanach Cottage, which had been Prince Charlie's headquarters, the Well of the Dead where the men of Clan Chattan fought with particular heroism, and King's Stables Cottage, where Cumberland's dragoons were picketed after the battle. At the same time Hector Forbes sold to the Trust a piece of land which contained the Cumberland Stone. It is said that the Duke stood on this rock as he directed the battle, but in fact he was on horseback. Ian Munro, the son of Alexander, made a further gift of land in 1959. In that year also Leanach Cottage became the first Culloden Visitor Centre.

Until the Trust's involvement the site had been cared for by the Gaelic Society of Inverness and a local committee, but with increasing numbers of visitors this was becoming a heavy responsibility. Part of the Trust's first commitment was to make provision for visitors and provide interpretation of the battle and its background. With local support and a grant and loan from the Highlands and Islands Development Board a new Culloden Centre was built and opened in 1970, on the anniversary of the battle. It was the first visitor centre to make use of audio-visual equipment. Two years later the Trust was able to purchase a modern bungalow which had most incongruously been built in the 1930s between Old Leanach and the memorial cairn. The Trust's first action was to have it demolished.

Culloden illustrates one of the Trust's more constructive yet continuing problems, the problem of success. With more to attract the public more visitors arrived, with a consequent need to increase provision for them. The Trust was able to acquire an additional part of the battlefield from the Forestry Commission, with grant aid from the Countryside Commission for Scotland and other charitable trusts. A further major redevelopment followed. With support from the local authority the road bisecting the battlefield was re-routed. Trees were felled, and the Visitor Centre and services to the public were extended. This ambitious transformation, which opened in 1984, was made possible by a grant from the EEC Community Fund.

Culloden is not only one of the Trust's most important and evocative historic sites, it is also linked with many other Trust properties. The Mackenzies of Kintail and the Macdonalds of Glencoe were amongst the clans at Culloden. John Irvine of Drum was there, and Charles Fraser commanded the Fraser Regiment. He was found wounded on the battlefield by General Hawley who ordered a young officer, James Wolfe, to kill him. Wolfe refused, but this did not save Charles: a less fastidious soldier was found to carry out the deed. Thirteen years later Charles's younger brother Simon died at Quebec, fighting under the same James Wolfe, by that time a general. Wolfe's experience at Culloden probably contributed to his assessment of Highland soldiers as 'hardy [and] intrepid', but expendable. Alexander, fifth Earl of Kellie, actively supported the Jacobite cause, and became a colonel in the Prince's army. He, too, fought at Culloden.

The estate of Fyvie had been bought by William Gordon, second Earl of Aberdeen, in 1733. His third wife was Lady Anne Gordon, sister of Lord Lewis Gordon, a member of Prince Charles Edward's council. He followed the Prince into exile. Lady Anne's husband died in 1745, but the next year she and her young son William watched the Duke of Cumberland ride by on his way to Aberdeen. When the Duke asked who she was she did not hesitate to reply that she was the sister of Lord Lewis Gordon, a notorious Jacobite. By the time William had grown up the Jacobite cause was beyond resuscitation. He himself became a general in the army of George III. But he had no wish to relinquish the heroic tradition of the Highlands, and the famous portrait painted by Pompeo Batoni shows him in a pose that grafts this tradition to that of classical heroes, dressed in tartan that is more like a toga than a plaid. The painting is one of the most prized features of Fyvie Castle.

Culloden saw the last battle to be fought on British soil and the end not only of the Jacobite resistance but of the predominantly feudal ways of the Highlands. The changes that followed were the consequences in part of devastation, in part of reconstruction. None of the areas in the Highlands in which the Trust has an involvement was untouched by the

Colonel William Gordon of Fyvie by Pompeo Baloni.

events of the Forty Five and their aftermath. The great castles of Aberdeenshire, on the edge of the Highlands, were also affected, whether the succeeding decades brought struggle or expansion. The Jacobites were not forgotten, but Scotland as a whole was ready for new directions and developments.

Haddo House.

CHAPTER SIX

Transformations

FOR many families north of the Highland Line life after Culloden would never be the same. Following the savage government reprisals came a period of both collapse and renewal: the collapse of a traditional way of life that had seemed organic to the landscape and its demands, and reconstruction, in part the delayed effects of the Union of 1707. The process had in fact begun long before 1707. Although the Union had some negative economic consequences, and these had bred support for the Jacobites, the renewal of progress in agriculture and trade, and an unprecedented acceleration of productivity in manufactures eventually made the Union acceptable. A receptivity to new ideas had been characteristic of the Scots aristocracy, both Jacobite and Whig, since before 1700.

The vitality of Scottish culture had reawakened with the relative stability of the second half of the seventeenth century. In architecture it no longer seemed necessary to put up fortifications. The 'old fashion of tours and castles', as the Earl of Strathmore put it, was no longer in favour, 'for who can delight to live in his house as in a prisone?' In the late seventeenth century the man most responsible for introducing Scotland to new architectural ideas was Sir William Bruce, Surveyor Royal to Charles II and James VII. Through his designs for the rebuilt Holyroodhouse Palace and the Duke of Lauder's Thirlestane Castle he demonstrated some of the possibilities of neo-classicism. He also designed the original Hopetoun House, which was extended by William Adam, and then worked on by William's son Robert. In 1731 William Gordon, second Earl of Aberdeen, had engaged William Adam, who had worked with Bruce, to design a new house to replace the tower house which had been the Gordon home since the fifteenth century.

The Earl of Aberdeen's new home, Haddo House, was a relatively modest residence, although the Gordons had been an influential family in the area for centuries, having estates at Methlick, Haddo and Kellie in Angus. Like other families in the north-east they had been caught up in the political and religious struggles of the seventeenth century. John Gordon had been second-in-command in the Marquess of Huntly's royalist forces, and in 1645 was taken prisoner. He was executed in Edinburgh. His son, another John, became Lord High Chancellor of Scotland in 1682, and was created Earl of Aberdeen. In the following decades the family had strong Jacobite associations, but managed to avoid direct involvement. It is unlikely that they would have been able to afford a new home if their Jacobite sympathies had led them to the battlefield.

The house is a pleasingly simple, symmetrical building on the model of the sixteenth-century Italian architect Palladio, who had revived classical styles. Adam himself was one of the chief eighteenth-century exponents of this reaction to the Baroque, although his interiors were often elaborate. Lord Aberdeen had decided views on what he wanted. The building was supervised by John Baxter, who had worked for Sir John Clerk of Penicuik, and took several years to complete. Haddo House may have been plain in style, especially in comparison with earlier country houses south of the Border, but it was an astonishing departure for a rural area usually regarded as distant from the centres of culture. Not so many years earlier Craigievar and improvements at Drum were still mindful of a tradition of raiding and warfare – and with good cause. Now, in the 1730s with contention still in the air, a house was built which linked status with comfort and elegance rather than the ability to defend and attack. In terms of local expectations the development was revolutionary.

Haddo remained with the Gordon family. George Gordon, the third Earl, was a somewhat unorthodox character who in addition to his official family at Haddo had several others installed in various residences. These arrangements were a severe drain on his finances. Nevertheless, for his son George, Lord Haddo, he bought the castle of Gight from Catherine Gordon, second wife of Captain John Byron and mother of another George Gordon, who became better known as Lord Byron. Lord Haddo was killed in 1791 by a fall from his horse. The next George Gordon, the fourth Earl, had a distinguished political career, becoming Prime Minister in 1852. The house was added to and enlarged, particularly in the early nineteenth century, when the very run-down house and grounds were put to rights. In 1880 there were additions and modifications, carried out by the Edinburgh architects Wardrop and Reid, and the London interior designers Wright and Mansfield. In 1881 a chapel was built designed by G E Street, a leading Gothic Revival architect, responsible for a number of ecclesiastical buildings as well as the Royal Courts of Justice in London.

Haddo House came to the Trust in 1978 from the Gordon family, with a generous endowment, and after necessary refurbishment it was opened to the public in 1979. In the same year the policies were opened as a Country Park by Grampian Regional Council, to be run as a co-operative venture between the Trust and Grampian Region. The Trust has rehabilitated the house to illustrate both its eighteenth-century origins and its late Victorian qualities.

The Gordons bring another of the Trust's houses onto the scene – Fyvie Castle. In 1733 when the second Earl was still engaged in building Haddo he also bought Fyvie, for his third wife Lady Anne Gordon. Their son William Gordon, who had stood with his mother to watch the passing of Cumberland's troops, began improvements to the castle in 1777, adding another tower and landscaping the parkland. William

The gardens at Haddo House.

The 1880 Entrance Hall of Haddo House.

The Ante Room, the original entrance hall of Haddo House.

Haddo House, North Quadrant Corridor.

Gordon was probably influenced by his travels in Europe in 1766. It was when he was in Rome that he commissioned the portrait by Batoni, and the heroic style may have fired an enthusiasm for improving Fyvie. The year after the opening of Haddo House a second William Adam house came to the Trust, as a bequest from Mrs M A A Lovett of Montrose. The bequest consisted of the House of Dun with its contents, two farms and several hundred acres of land, including twenty-five acres of woodland. The Trust could not have taken on the House of Dun without the enthusiastic response to a rather unusual appeal, which asked for donations to individual rooms of the house. The public were attracted by the prospect of their contributions going to specific aspects of restoration, and the appeal exceeded its target, enabling an enthusiastic and meticulous programme of restoration.

Dun, near Montrose, was originally bought by Sir Robert Erskine in 1375, and the Erskines remained lairds of Dun, playing their part both locally and nationally. Sir John Erskine, whose father, grandfather, uncle and great-uncle were all killed at Flodden, was a particularly distinguished member of the family, a man of learning and influence

*Augustus John Kennedy Erskine, the 19th Laird, in
the courtyard House of Dun.*

*Millicent Erskine (Mrs. Lovett) with her sister
Marjorie.*

Detail of Joseph Enzer's plasterwork in the Saloon, House of Dun.

who was highly respected during the time of Mary, Queen of Scots. David Erskine, for whom Adam designed the new house, was a leading Scottish judge.

Adam's design adapted a plan originally prepared by the Jacobite Earl of Mar, and it is a more embellished structure than Haddo, though it also dates from 1730. Its most striking features are the recessed arched entrance and the large saloon. In the early nineteenth century there were extensive alterations, which left only four rooms, including the saloon, intact. In more recent years the house was let as an hotel. Although there had been some alterations, and the needs of an hotel are clearly different from those of a private house, a large amount of the fittings and furniture survived.

For the Trust the House of Dun has entailed one of its most ambitious and satisfying recent conservation projects. Much work had to be done initially to the policies, the courtyard of the house and its buildings which were in a particularly dilapidated state. In 1987 work started on the house itself, beginning with the re-slating and re-leading of the roof. Other work on the exterior of the building included refacing the south elevation with carefully matched stone and replacing glazing bars on the windows. It was also decided to erect balustrades on the north and south fronts, which were part of Adam's design but had never been built.

Inside the house the objective has been to allow the expression of the original disposition of the house, underplaying the furnishings, but where necessary supplying accurate reproductions of certain features. Where appropriate rooms have been restored to their original configuration, particularly the Library which had been divided into bedrooms and closets. Paintwork has been returned to sympathetic colours and wallpaper sensitively chosen. Investigation brought to light a number of original features that had been lost in subsequent alterations. With ingenuity and imagination the restoration made use of

Restoring the 18th-century plasterwork in the Saloon, House of Dun.

The Red Bedroom, House of Dun.

surviving features, and every clue to the house's original nature was followed up. An example is the survival of a few Delft tiles of the 1740s which made it possible to make copies for the two fireplaces in the saloon. A pair of eighteenth-century firedogs fortuitously acquired by the curator some years before came into their own. A second pair was cast, and the two pairs now also occupy the fireplaces. Other reproductions include carpets woven to original patterns.

The rehabilitation of the House of Dun shows what can be achieved with care, sensitivity and enthusiasm, and a fair measure of inventiveness and opportunism. It was an exciting and rewarding project to which many contributed. In parallel with the restoration programme the Trust was able to refurbish two flats over the stable block which are now let as holiday accommodation: another illustration of the policy of giving new life to old buildings.

The current of improvement reached Leith Hall in the 1750s, when John Leith was adding to the house. The Leith family had been strong Jacobites, but although five of his uncles had taken up arms John himself, at fourteen, was too young to fight, and his father had died before the Forty Five. John Leith built a new wing along the east side of the courtyard and a new kitchen. The stables were rebuilt, and later improvements were made to the estate. The latter were carried out by John Leith's widow Harriet Stuart, a woman of strength and initiative who ran the estate after her husband had been killed in a quarrel. She was helped by Andrew Hay, John's uncle, who returned to his home at Rannes in 1763 after years of exile for his part in the Forty Five. Being well over seven feet tall he was a conspicuous Jacobite in every sense of the word.

For Harriet Stuart the running of Leith Hall and the bringing up of her three sons, the eldest of whom was consumptive and died at the age of nineteen, was a constant struggle. When Harriet died in 1780 the debts had mounted, for Alexander, her second son, serving in the army, maintained an extravagant lifestyle. Before long he was facing the prospect of selling Leith Hall. He was rescued by his great-uncle Andrew, who in 1789 sold his own home at Rannes and bought Leith Hall, which he then returned to Alexander Leith, free of debt. The laird of Leith Hall became Alexander Leith-Hay, and his first son was called Andrew. Andrew Hay died shortly after making this magnanimous gesture.

The fortunes of Alexander changed dramatically. A cousin left him a plantation in the West Indies worth £29,000. His military career flourished and he became a general. In the 1790s he was in a position to extend the house again, doubling its size and giving it a new elegance, both inside and out. He persuaded his tenants into improved methods of agriculture which increased the productiveness of the estate. His brother James also became a general, seeing service in the West Indies and in the Peninsular War, along with the thousands of soldiers drafted

Volunteer restorers at work on textiles for the House of Dun.

Culzean Castle.

The Saloon, Culzean Castle.

into the Scottish regiments formed after the Jacobite threat had faded. Alexander's son Andrew served as his aide-de-camp, and both participated in the siege of San Sebastian in 1813. Andrew was a man of more than military talents, and had a later career as politician, writer and painter. But he was, like his father, extravagant, and when he inherited Leith Hall in 1838, by that time as Sir Andrew Leith-Hay, he could not at first afford to live there. Debt and diminished economic circumstances did not go well with improved residences.

Sir Andrew's son Alexander Sebastian (after the siege) continued the family tradition of service in the army. He fought in the Crimea, one of the 'thin red streak' at Balaclava, and in India, where he led the 93rd Sutherland Highlanders to raise the siege of Lucknow. Amongst the spoils he brought back to Leith Hall were items from the household of the Nawab of Oudh and a Hindustani-speaking parrot. The distinguished military careers of the Leith family are illustrated in a collection displayed by the Trust at Leith Hall.

There was striking evidence of transformation in other parts of Scotland. On the Ayrshire coast the ancient stronghold of the powerful Kennedy family was inherited in 1744 by Sir Thomas Kennedy. Culzean Castle was at that time an uncompromising fortified keep set on a cliff top, rather the worse for wear, and with estates that had received little attention. He embarked on some improvements to the house, including a new wing built out between the castle and the sea. But perhaps more important was his work on the estate. Agricultural improvement was very much in the air and growing numbers of landowners were experimenting, and encouraging their tenants to try out some of the new ideas. Sir Thomas enclosed the land, much of which was barren heath, and introduced crop rotation and the use of fertilizers. He planted trees to provide shelter, and built roads to improve communications. Enclosure meant the displacement of people, so he built the village of Straiton to accommodate those who were uprooted, and encouraged them in handloom weaving. The linen industry in Scotland had benefited from the Union, which had opened up English markets for Scottish cloth, and at that time the future of the handloom weavers seemed assured.

All this activity cost money, of course, but it was an excellent investment. In 1762 Sir Thomas inherited the title of Earl of Cassillis, but he preferred to continue living at Culzean rather than take up residence in the more prestigious seat of Cassillis. In 1775 his brother David, a successful Edinburgh lawyer, became the tenth Earl and soon embarked on further extensions. He called in Robert Adam, son of William, who had spent a considerable time on the Continent and in England studying classical and neo-classical architecture, to plan modifications to the castle. Adam's first plan of 1777 involved modest alterations to the house, but before long the scheme escalated. New

The Oval Staircase, Culzean Castle.

The Camellia House, one of the many small buildings in the grounds of Culzean Castle.

Culzean Castle.

rooms were added, with a grand staircase and more emphasis on the turrets. Then a round tower and bedrooms were added to the wing Sir Thomas had built.

The next phase of the building came in 1785. Now Sir Thomas's wing was demolished and in its place an impressive drum tower was built on the edge of the cliff, still Culzean's most distinctive feature on the seaward side. Its centrepiece was a large and stylish saloon. Culzean is one of Robert Adam's triumphs, for it combines with grace and originality classical proportion and romantic fluidity. The picturesque elements are not just embellishments, but are an organic part of the whole. The interior, for which Adam was also responsible, was decorated and furnished to conform with the growing emphasis on grace and comfort. The proportions of rooms, the colours and the ornamentation were all integral to the overall effect. Adam also designed numerous outbuildings, most notably the farm steading. Some of the other buildings are more ornamental than functional, but they all contribute to the impact of Culzean as a total environment.

In 1945 the Trust was preparing itself for action again in the wake of the Second World War when it was faced with a decision of huge dimensions. It had already established a reputation for judicious risk-taking: now there came a proposal that represented simultaneously immense potential and alarming responsibility. It came in the form of an offer from the fifth Marquess of Ailsa (the twelfth Earl of Cassillis had

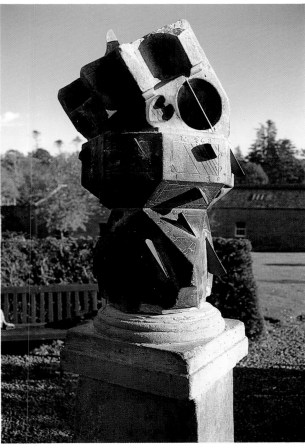

become Marquess of Ailsa in 1831), the offer of Culzean Castle. The proposed gift of a magnificent house, one of the great achievements of one of Scotland's greatest architects, which was in considerable need of repair, was without an endowment to help with the cost of conservation and maintenance.

Ever since the Trust made the courageous decision to accept this offer the survival of Culzean has depended on public response to the many appeals that have been launched on its behalf. An initial appeal raised £20,000, which with another £20,000 from the government and support from the Pilgrim Trust enabled the start of urgent conservation work. Other appeals have been launched regularly, as restoration and the massive campaign against erosion continue. For Culzean pays dearly for its dramatic clifftop setting. The salt- and sand-laden winds attack the local honey-coloured sandstone, which has been gently crumbling since the eighteenth century. A challenging task for the Trust has been the part-replacement of the outer skin of stone, on the house itself and on the numerous outbuildings. The work of conservation has been going on for nearly half a century, and will need to continue for the foreseeable future. It covers not only the numerous buildings, but the extensive grounds.

There have been many partners in this conservation campaign, including the Historic Buildings Council for Scotland, Strathclyde Regional Council, the Countryside Commission for Scotland, Kyle and Carrick District, and the thousands of individuals who have contributed in cash and in kind. Restoration of the interior was equally a challenge, perhaps the biggest the Trust has taken on. Deliberate alteration and inevitable deterioration – for much of the castle had not been lived in for a long time – had masked the nature of Adam's achievement, which had shown an impressive range and flexibility. A rescue operation was needed, which involved considerable dedication and research.

Part of the agreement between the Trust and the Kennedy family was that a flat should be established on the top floor, and the tenancy of this was offered to General Dwight D Eisenhower, Supreme Commander of Allied Forces in Europe, as a gesture of gratitude. General Eisenhower accepted the offer, and visited Culzean for the first time in the autumn of 1946. He took a great interest in the castle and the project to restore it. It was some time before the full dimensions of the task were appreciated, but work got under way at once, and by May 1947, when Culzean opened to the public, rehabilitation was far enough advanced for some of the castle, at least, to be ready to receive visitors.

A full restoration programme for the interior began in 1972, and for ten years was a major focus of the Trust's effort. Adam's drawings for the interior were found, which, with the taking of paint scrapes, helped to establish the original colour schemes. The pale blue and green which predominate underline the influence on the castle's character of the sea

The new carpet for the Saloon at Culzean Castle, woven locally to the original pattern.

on the one hand and the countryside on the other. There was no attempt to force any of the rooms back to their original aspect: for example, Adam's library and adjacent dressing room had in the nineteenth century been refurbished as a large dining room, and its Victorian character has been maintained. Adam's eating room is now a small sitting room. Where necessary fittings were carefully researched and reconstructed. Surviving fittings were meticulously conserved: the balusters of the dramatic oval staircase were each dismantled and cleaned, as were the arms of the West Lowland Fencibles, the volunteer regiment that had been raised by the twelfth Earl of Cassillis in case of invasion by Napoleon. The latter were worked on by one of the many teams of young trainees which have done invaluable work for the Trust, and in some cases have introduced their members to a highly skilled and satisfying career. The huge circular carpet in the saloon was too worn to retain, but the Trust arranged for a copy to be woven locally. Like the other reconstructions it is the result of scrupulous craftsmanship.

Most of the original furniture moved with the Kennedy family when they left Culzean for Cassillis, so another major feature of the restoration programme has been the acquisition of suitable re-placements. Many items have been donated or loaned. Others have come to Culzean through the Treasury in lieu of death duties. Many of the Trust's properties have benefited from the alert and opportunistic action of its staff in acquiring appropriate material, both in the saleroom

The Swan Pond Court, Culzean Castle.

and from less orthodox sources. Whatever the source, the policy is to furnish with sympathy rather than pedantry.

The stonework dominates current work at Culzean and the conservation programme is concentrating on the fifty or so small buildings which are a unique feature of the estate. To facilitate the work the Trust is to set up its own stonemason's workshop at Culzean. This implements a policy to provide more in-house conservation services. Until now the Trust's workshop in Edinburgh has handled metalwork conservation and replica-making, but it is hoped that in the future, and in collaboration with other heritage organizations, more workshops will follow. The pooling of resources and skills will increase the effectiveness of this initiative.

The needs of Culzean's environs have been demanding in a different way. Culzean Country Park, Scotland's first country park, has been in existence since 1969, and is managed by the Trust for Strathclyde Regional Council and the District Councils of Kyle and Carrick, and Cumnock and Doon Valley. It is the most visited of all the Trust's properties. In 1973 the Culzean Country Park Centre opened in the converted Home Farm buildings. The grounds include formal gardens, parklands, wild and planted woodland, the Swan Pond, the Deer Park, farmland and the shore itself. Without the ranger service, a 1970 initiative with far-reaching implications, it would be impossible to cope with the 300,000 or so visitors who come every year. The rangers' dual role of conservation and education has been particularly effective with the young, who have made their own very practical contribution to the conservation effort, but is also much appreciated by older visitors.

The sympathetic refurbishment of the farm steading and grounds was the result of the advice and work of the landscape architect Elizabeth Beazley, who recognized that old buildings and old spaces could be put to new uses without damaging their character. The Trust has continually benefited from the help and advice of experts and specialists in many fields. An imaginative approach to the function of Trust properties has been essential, for viability depends on maintaining buildings and land as working entities. The Guest Flat in Culzean Castle is a good example. It now provides conference and meeting facilities as well as comfortable accommodation for numerous organizations and individuals, from the UK and abroad.

Culzean blends the enlightened and energetic achievement of eighteenth-century Scotland with a very practical demonstration of what conservation of both the natural and the fabricated environment can accomplish. It is an emblem on a large scale and in particularly dramatic circumstances of what in their different ways each of the Trust properties embodies. But if Culzean represents the picturesque side of Robert Adam's talent and of Scotland's Age of Enlightenment, equally important were the more sober urban developments. Another of the Trust's properties expresses this aspect of Scotland's growth in the second half of the eighteenth century, and at the same time is a reminder of some of the less happy consequences of the Jacobite Risings.

In 1796 John Lamont, eighteenth chief of Clan Lamont, was granted the feu of 7 Charlotte Square in Edinburgh and made arrangements to purchase the new house that was going up there. Lamont was one of many small chieftains and landowners whose response to inevitable changes in the Highlands was to escape. He spent little time at Ardlamont in Argyll, his family home, preferring the attractions of London and Edinburgh. He financed this lifestyle by the introduction of sheep onto his land, more profitable than the tenants who were thereby displaced, and by the rents of those tenants who remained.

If John Lamont's actions as an absentee landlord were symptomatic of a current of change in the Highlands, his acquisition of 7 Charlotte Square was equally illustrative of another aspect of transformation. The northward expansion of the city of Edinburgh in the second half of the eighteenth century was dramatic not just visually but in its effect on life in the capital city. The overcrowding of Edinburgh's Old Town had for a long time been seen as requiring urgent action, and by the middle of the eighteenth century there was considerable debate about the form that action should take. The old tenements were in many cases not only insalubrious, but dangerously dilapidated. In addition to the recognition of the practical difficulties and consequences of cramming a large number of people into a restricted space, there was a feeling that

Edinburgh's citizens deserved more gracious surroundings. The city had few impressive and ornamental public buildings, few of the embellishments that, some felt, were appropriate to a capital.

There were attempts to rectify this within and to the south of the Old Town. Some new buildings went up, the Royal Exchange (now the City Chambers) and St Cecilia's Hall, for example, and George Square, but there was only one possibility for a radical solution, and that was to the north. To accomplish it the first step was the draining of the Nor' Loch, which was begun in 1759, and the construction of a bridge and 'a road of communication' between the High Street and the area to the north and on to Leith. Work began on the bridge in 1766. In the same year the Town Council invited architects to 'make plans of regular streets and buildings' to be put up on the fields that would soon be linked with the Old Town.

The plan chosen for Edinburgh's 'New Town' was that by James Craig, a young architect who produced in 1767 a grid arrangement of streets and squares with green space and room for 'stately' buildings as well as terraces of houses. There were several architects involved in the building of the New Town, and playing a leading role were Robert and James Adam. It was Robert Adam who designed the north side of Charlotte Square, including numbers 5, 6 and 7. The houses began to go up after 1792.

All three houses now belong to the Trust. They came to the Trust in 1966 after the death of their owner, the fifth Marquess of Bute, having been accepted by the Commissioners of Inland Revenue in part satisfaction of Estate Duty. But the Trust's involvement with Charlotte Square goes back much further, for since 1949 the Trust had leased number 5, originally feued to the Grants of Rothiemurchus, for use as its headquarters. Number 6 is now leased as the official residence of the Secretary of State for Scotland. The upper floors of number 7 were converted, with the support of the Baird Trust, into a flat for use as the Edinburgh residence of the Moderator of the General Assembly of the Church of Scotland. Thus the Trust is landlord to the heads of church and state who, on occasion at least, are neighbours.

The movement from the congested Old Town to the spacious New began slowly in the 1770s, but soon built up speed. There was an initial reluctance to take up residence in large, airy houses with open outlooks after the necessarily intimate lifestyle imposed by the Old Town. Inevitably, the move meant a change in social habits. The easy informality and homely socializing were replaced by a more refined style of social intercourse and more defined attitudes to social class. By the early nineteenth century, which saw the second phase of the New Town going up, all those who could afford the move were keen to descend to its desirable residences. The Old Town was abandoned to a decline that rapidly produced the decayed slums that efforts were made to rescue in the 1930s and after. The Trust's Gladstone's Land remains an impressive illustration of the result of these efforts.

John Lamont was not part of the exodus from the Old Town, but nevertheless an instance of the increasing draw of the New. For country lairds who wanted to set themselves up in town it was the new Edinburgh that offered the elegant lifestyle that was an important part of the attraction. Lamont occupied number 7 until 1815, when the house was sold to Mrs Catherine Farquharson of Invercauld. Thirty years later it was bought by Charles Neaves, a successful Edinburgh advocate who became a judge, Lord Neaves, after the death of his neighbour Lord Cockburn, whose town house was 14 Charlotte Square. From 1889 number 7 was the home of the Reverend Alexander Whyte, minister of St George's West and Moderator of the Free Church General Assembly in 1898, and later Principal of New College. The house was bought by the Marquess of Bute in 1927.

When 7 Charlotte Square came to the Trust it was being leased by Whytock & Reid, a firm of antique dealers and furnishers. When their lease expired in 1973 the decision was made to rehabilitate three floors in the Georgian style of the original house. When the Charlotte Square houses were built, although the exteriors conformed to Adam's design the interior design varied according to the wishes of the purchasers. The inside of number 7 was rather plain, perhaps because John Lamont did not have a great deal of money to spend.

The aim of the Trust was to recreate a typical Georgian town house, and this has been accomplished with infinite care and attention to detail. Many of the original features had disappeared, for example the drawing-room fireplace, and others had been incongruously added. Amongst the many tasks of restoration were the removal of a Victorian cornice and the reinstatement of appropriate Adam colours. The basement kitchen is now one of the major attractions of the house, but in 1973 nothing of the original kitchen survived, and its reconstruction was both a challenge and a delight. Gradually the necessary furnishings, utensils and equipment were acquired, and an authentic Georgian kitchen was pieced together.

This kind of loving and meticulous recreation is characteristic of the Trust's work. It requires flair and imagination and an intimate understanding of the property concerned as well as expert knowledge. Success depends on getting the feel of a place right and finding the best way to express it, without being pedantic about detail. The Georgian House is full of fascinating detail, but it also gives a lively impression of Georgian Edinburgh, a city that was at the height of its cultural achievement, a beacon of learning and intellectual enquiry throughout Europe. For many the planning and architecture of the New Town was a symbol of this achievement, and some of the best-known figures of the Scottish Enlightenment lived in the squares and crescents that continued to spread northwards down the hill and to the east and west until the middle of the nineteenth century.

The Kitchen, the Georgian House, Charlotte Square, Edinburgh.

The Scullery, the Georgian House.

The Georgian House provides an ideal educational focus for learning about this most dramatic chapter in Edinburgh's social and architectural history. For the general public the volunteer staff can fill in the details of the house and its history, but in addition the Trust's Education Department runs projects for schools which give pupils an invaluable insight into life in Georgian Edinburgh. There is no substitute for the direct experience of the interiors and artefacts of another age, and visits to the house itself are backed up with audio-visual and printed material which invite an imaginative response from children. Education programmes at the Georgian House complement those at Gladstone's Land where there is an education room and visiting classes can experiment with dressing-up and role-play. Between them the two houses illustrate two crucial centuries of Edinburgh's past.

The ideas of the Enlightenment may have originated in the closes and taverns of the Old Town, where academics and artists, lawyers and literati gathered and debated, but they reached maturity in the more formal environment of the New Town, consciously conceived as a symbol of a new age. The grid pattern that widened into squares and was deliberately broken by angles and crescents was an emblem of reason and the rational arrangement of space. The topography itself, the steep slope down to the Water of Leith, the drama of the High Street skyline, and the expansive vista across the Firth of Forth were reminders of nature and the response of feeling. The distinguished figures that made their way from medieval coalescence to Georgian discrimination, men such as David Hume, did so in the belief that the move represented an advance for reason and for Scotland.

The spirit of improvement touched many lives and many homes, and its effects are illustrated by Trust properties in many small ways as well as through the great achievements of Culzean and Charlotte Square. Half a century after Culloden the face of Scotland was undergoing many changes. New ways of farming, new crops, enclosure, new attitudes towards the breeding of livestock, transformed the landscape. While existing houses were being improved and new houses built for the wealthy, new villages were planned and constructed for farm workers and fisher folk. New ways of harnessing power were beginning to have revolutionary effects on industry. In the first half of the eighteenth century Scotland experienced political and military struggle against the background of her uneasy political union with England. It also saw the initiation of new ideas in art, science and industry, which flourished in the more stable conditions after 1750. The next century would see the often dramatic consequences of some of these beginnings.

CHAPTER SEVEN

Agriculture and Industry

ULZEAN Castle and the fine new houses in Charlotte Square illustrate how, for a minority, expectations and possibilities changed in the second half of the eighteenth century. But these new developments were dependent on other changes: on an expanding economy and the contributing increase in agricultural and industrial production. Although Edinburgh's New Town and the Adam family's country houses were conspicuous signs of transformation they were not necessarily the most dramatic. The land itself was changing, and with it a way of life which the majority of Scotland's population had for centuries taken for granted. Expectations and possibilities changed for many.

The horizons of Scotland's lairds and landowners were extending, both inside and out. They now expected new standards of comfort in their homes. There was no need for self-defence or self-sufficiency. Materials and furnishings were imported – or if the objects themselves were not imports the ideas and designs often were. The relaxation and extension of the old fortified houses required interiors that were both more comfortable and more elaborate than the rather spartan environment inherited from times of raid and siege. These improvements affected not just the material environment, but dress and behaviour, language, and food and drink. One of the results of the Union of 1707 was a sensitive, perhaps over-sensitive, awareness of differences between England and Scotland. English visitors were often rather disparaging about Scottish ways. Many Scots now consciously set out to cultivate a more sophisticated style, turning to England and the Continent for exemplars of taste and behaviour.

Much of this is reflected in the Trust's properties, not only in extended and refurbished buildings but in the way the estates were laid out and run. The new castle of Culzean was part of a whole, the reorganization of the estates essential to both the vision and the functioning of the house. Adam's design of the Home Farm and outbuildings underlines this. To sustain a splendid new house the estates had to be profitable, and to be profitable it was necessary to introduce new techniques of raising both crops and animals. But also it was felt desirable that the landscape, like the home, should be arranged in a pleasing and rational manner.

In 1792 Miss Elyza Fraser, sister of Charles Fraser who died at Culloden, inherited Castle Fraser and set to work to make improvements. In addition to leaving the building 'Restored and Beautified' she embarked on an ambitious project to landscape the

Fyvie Loch.

Fyvie Castle.

policies. The landscape gardener Thomas White was asked to provide plans for redesigning, some of which were carried out, in Miss Elyza's lifetime and later. Her companion Mary Bristow took an active interest in these improvements, and was responsible for planting a grove of trees. Elyza Fraser's great-nephew Colonel Charles Mackenzie Fraser inherited on her death in 1814, and continued the work. He was much inspired by the example of Sir Archibald Grant of Monymusk, also in Aberdeenshire, one of the leading agricultural improvers of the time. Grant was a Member of Parliament (before being expelled for corruption) and in close contact with English improving landowners. He was ruthless in his treatment of his tenants, but there is no indication that Charles Mackenzie Fraser followed him in that.

The object of improvement was to make better use of the land. It involved bringing more land under the plough, a more extensive use of fertilizer, especially lime to re-nourish sour, exhausted soil, and the introduction of new crops. The digging of drainage systems, the supplanting of the old runrig system by enclosure, necessary both to define areas of planting and to control livestock, and the practice of crop rotation were all essential features of improvement. The Lothians had been in the forefront of these developments since the late seventeenth century, but before long landowners all along the east coast were experimenting, and Fife, Angus and Aberdeenshire all saw the introduction of new ideas and techniques.

The clock at Fyvie Castle.

Charles Mackenzie Fraser was an enthusiastic improver, both in the immediate environs of the castle, where he built a walled garden for growing fruit and vegetables, and further afield. Amongst the changes he instigated to the castle itself was the building of a grand double staircase lit by a cupola, and of two gatehouses. Other developments reflected a change in lifestyle: the Great Hall was refurbished as a drawing room and two rooms were combined to form a library.

The Jacobite involvements of the Setons of Fyvie meant that the estate was forfeit, and in 1733 it was sold by the Crown to the second Earl of Aberdeen, which established the link between Fyvie and Haddo. William Gordon, Lord Aberdeen's son and subject of Batoni's portrait, carried out a number of improvements to the estate towards the end of the century, when soaring agricultural prices made improvement highly profitable. The parkland still retains the character that it acquired at that time. The marsh that had once had a defensive function was drained to make an ornamental loch, the grounds landscaped and trees planted. William Gordon's son, another William, carried on the work, and recorded that he had enclosed and planted two hundred acres of land, building dykes, planting hedges and putting in roads – all the recognized ingredients of improvement. He went on, 'The garden has been laid out and enlarged and has been filled with the most expensive flowers, evergreens, and fruit trees; and a large sum has been expended in bringing a steady and abundant supply of water to the lakes within the grounds.'

The younger William inherited Fyvie in 1816. While he was energetically at work his relative George, the fourth Earl (he was the great-grandson of the second Earl of Aberdeen and his second wife Lady Susan Murray, while William was the grandson of the Earl and his third wife Lady Anne Gordon) was rescuing Haddo House from decay. George Gordon was only seven years old when he inherited Haddo, and was brought up mainly in England. It was 1805 before he returned to Haddo, to find it in an almost ruinous state. The policies were bare of trees and peat moss had crept across the grounds from the margins. The house itself, unlived in for years, was 'of appalling badness', and the task of reclamation that faced Lord Aberdeen was formidable. However, he set about it with conviction. In spite of the considerable demands of his political career he devoted a great deal of effort throughout the rest of his life to restoring Haddo, which just a few decades earlier had been such a splendid symbol of the new age.

Lord Aberdeen was not content with making the house habitable and tidying up the estate. He did more than restore – he improved. He cleared the peat moss, and planted huge numbers of trees – fourteen million altogether. With the help of James Giles, the Aberdeen artist and landscape designer, he landscaped the grounds, putting in ornamental lakes and laying out flower beds and formal drives as well as more rustic walks. It was a gradual process. In 1833 he was still finding

The Entrance Hall, Fyvie Castle.

Haddo depressing – 'the gloom and desolation of the place can scarcely be endured', he wrote in a letter to his children. But he carried on, and derived satisfaction from each piece of work accomplished. He was attentive to the estate as well as to the immediate grounds, building new farmhouses and bringing farming practices up to date.

Another phase of improvement began at the end of the century. The sixth Earl of Aberdeen had opted for an adventurous and incognito life at sea, which claimed his life. His brother John inherited and he and his wife, Ishbel Marjoribanks, set about modernizing the house and the estate. Amongst the improvements, designed by Wardrop and Reid, was the installation of bathrooms. But the Aberdeens concerned themselves with much more than the physical environment. They organized committees and classes offering opportunities for education to the community, and arranged cultural events. It soon became clear that premises were necessary for all this activity, and a hall was built out of timber, Canadian-style. The cultural traditions of Haddo have been sustained, and the hall is now the home of the Haddo House Choral Society and the Haddo House Hall Arts Trust.

The Aberdeens were equally active on the larger stage of public life. Lord Aberdeen was Governor-General of Ireland and then of Canada, and then Viceroy in Ireland. In 1916 he was created Marquess of Aberdeen and Temair. The warmth and energy of the Marquess and his wife, who referred to themselves as 'We Twa', has been kept alive in

Haddo House by the equally spirited involvements of their descendants. June, Marchioness of Aberdeen, still lives in Haddo and continues the tradition.

The later eighteenth-century interest in landscaping was usually evidence of an urge to blend the natural with the more formal, rather than to impose order on nature. Earlier in the century there was a stronger emphasis on formality. The 1730s landscaped garden at Brodie Castle is an example. The scheme was devised by Alexander Brodie, and involved the planting of avenues of limes and beeches and an artificial pond, which still remains. Later, in Victorian times, another phase of planting illustrated the contemporary taste for exotic trees, but little of this now survives.

While eighteenth-century landscaping aimed to foster a sense of natural wildness and to create pleasing vistas and an agreeable environment, in an earlier period gardens of a spectacular formality had been established. The epitome of this can be found at Pitmedden, where in 1675 Sir Alexander Seton created his Great Garden, almost certainly inspired by French models and by the gardens of Sir William Bruce's extended Palace of Holyroodhouse. At that time formality dominated the arrangement of gardens, and where spaces were large there was scope for an elaborate diversity. The garden at Pitmedden was terraced, with pavilions at either end and stairs leading from the higher to the lower level.

Pitmedden came to the Trust in 1952 as a gift, with endowment, from Major James Keith. At that time what had once been Pitmedden's Great Garden was being used to grow vegetables. The reconstruction of the original garden has been a triumph of research and restoration, which involved a large number of people in dedicated work over a period of nearly twenty years. A key figure in its success was the late Dr James Richardson, formerly Inspector of Ancient Monuments in Scotland whose researches provided the basis for the design. Three of the garden's four parterres are taken from Gordon of Rothiemay's bird's eye drawings of the Holyroodhouse gardens, while the fourth is based on the coat-of-arms of Sir Alexander Seton. Thanks to Dr Richardson's detective work it was possible to redesign an authentic seventeenth-century garden, but the actual work of reconstruction remained. Much of this was achieved by Lady Elphinstone and a dedicated team who translated Dr Richardson's plan into horticultural reality. The planting of hundreds of yards of box hedge to mark the margins of the parterres was just a beginning. Now that the Trust has established the recreated garden the maintenance, involving the raising and planting out of 40,000 annual plants, continues to be an absorbing enterprise.

Pitmedden also played an important part in the process of agricultural improvement and that aspect of the estate has been acknowledged by the setting up of a Museum of Farming Life. This was made possible by the donation to the Trust of the collection of farm tools

The Great Garden of Pitmedden.

The north-east parterre, Pitmedden.

The Museum of Farming Life at Pitmedden.

and domestic artefacts made by the late Mr William Cook of Little Meldrum, a nearby farm. These provide a valuable record of local farming life in which the community takes an active interest. The Museum consists of a number of farm buildings and displays of farming equipment and domestic material. The recreation of farming interiors of the past provides a glimpse of the traditions that surround Pitmedden.

The well-being of Scotland east of the Grampians was dependent on agriculture, hand-loom weaving and the fisheries, and all three were supported and encouraged in different ways after the Union and after the Jacobite Risings. The Board of Trustees for Fisheries and Manufactures, set up in 1727, promoted rural industries and fishing. The commissioners who ran the estates of Jacobite sympathisers that were forfeited to the government promoted the improvement of farming methods. After the estates were returned to their original owners or heirs in 1784 part of this role was continued by the Highland Society of Edinburgh, later the Royal Highland and Agricultural Society, and the Board of Agriculture.

Any record of rural life in the late eighteenth and nineteenth centuries is bound to reflect these efforts towards making the countryside more productive. The activity of improvement began as a hobby motivated by public spirit and later became profitable. It owed much to organizations which promulgated the new ideas. These changes affected both the working and domestic lives of country people all over Scotland. Some tenants were displaced, others became implementers of the new techniques and ideas. Some were keen, others were given little choice by their landlords. The effect of improvement was to consolidate what had once been large numbers of small holdings into larger units. Although some displaced tenants took up other occupations, like the Culzean tenants who were moved to the new village of Straiton and became weavers, many became tenureless farm servants. Instead of being longterm tenants on an estate, subsistence farming a few acres of land, they were now hired annually or seasonally.

The Angus Folk Museum at Glamis illustrates many aspects of country life, of the eighteenth, nineteenth and early twentieth centuries. The Museum originated with the collecting enthusiasm of Jean, Lady Maitland. With her late husband, Sir Ramsay Maitland of Burnside, she gathered material relating to country life in Angus and in 1953 opened the Angus and District Folk Museum in the Manse at Rescobie, near Forfar. In 1955 the Angus Folk Collection Trust was formed. Soon the collection of domestic, agricultural and social historical material outgrew its premises. In 1957 the Earl of Strathmore offered Kirkwynd Cottages in Glamis to the National Trust for Scotland as premises for the Museum. These were five one-storey cottages and a communal wash-house, characteristic rural houses dating from the early nineteenth century. A successful appeal for funds made it possible to restore and adapt the cottages for their new purpose. Later that year the new Museum opened to the public.

Restoration work carried out by the Trust involved linking and re-roofing the cottages, and replacing the wooden floors with flagstones. One room has been refurbished as a cottage kitchen and another as a parlour in a Victorian manse. Collecting continued, and in 1976 an extension was opened, funded by an anonymous endowment from a resident of Angus. The extension was added specifically to display agricultural implements, and this is now an important focus of the Museum.

The Museum is characterized by objects that formed the material fabric of life and work in rural Angus. They are objects with which at one time many of the people of Angus would have had an intimate familiarity – cast iron kettles and girdles probably made in local foundries, candle moulds and cruisie lamps, spinning wheels and butter churns. Furniture was generally plain, although the manse parlour illustrates the Victorian concern for comfort and ornament. In the late eighteenth and early nineteenth centuries local trades expanded, responding to the needs of improving agriculture and increased building, and the increased purchasing power that resulted. Domestic utensils, pottery and some furniture would be locally made. Also locally made and serviced were farm implements, horse harness and the wealth of tools and gear required by the farmer.

As an illustration of Scotland's agricultural heritage the Angus Folk Museum is well placed. The county of Angus included rich arable land and a long stretch of sea coast which traditionally provided seaweed for fertilizer. With good harbours at Dundee, Arbroath and Montrose it was easy to export farm produce to the Continent of Europe. Good grazing on the slopes of the Sidlaw Hills gave Angus a reputation for stock rearing – Strathmore in Angus is the home of Aberdeen Angus cattle. To the north and west there is rougher grazing where Angus meets the encroaching Grampians. Up until the 1730s an open landscape stretched across the county, with few divisions and few roads. Communities were very local, largely self-sufficient in both supplies and skills. Apart from the movement of grain for export such goods as were traded were transported by packhorse, and the commonest means of getting from one place to another was on foot. Only the wealthiest landowners had carriages.

The process of improvement was gradual and very hard work. The sheer labour involved in clearing and draining land and preparing it for rotation crops was huge. The use of fertilizers, mainly lime, derived from burning limestone, and marl, mineral-rich silt, was vital. In response to the changes in land use came a revolution in farming technology, which brought more sophisticated implements, such as the swing plough developed by James Small, which came into use in the 1770s, and Patrick Bell's reaper of 1828. The new technology meant that fewer men could accomplish more in less time. But it also created work of a different kind. The new farming created a need for good roads, which required maintenance. The new machinery needed to be made and looked after. The hedger and the ditcher were kept busy. The smith had more work than before, shoeing the horses that replaced oxen as draught animals as well as repairing implements. There was increased work for the wheelwright, and the expansion of farm buildings kept joiners, masons, tilers and slaters busy. Trades also became more specialized, which in turn promoted contact between communities, for a single village was unlikely to provide every skill required. The farmer was less likely now to mend or replace his own horse harness, but would go to a saddler, perhaps some distance away, to get it done.

Much of this is documented in the Angus Folk Museum, which complements the stories told by the great houses and illustrates some of the effects of the new directions initiated by their owners. Linked with the whole process of change was the range of rural industries that developed in step with agricultural improvement. Prominent amongst these were the mills, where local farmers had their corn ground. Of the two mills in the Trust's care one, Barry Mill, is in Angus. It was purchased in 1988 with a bequest from Miss Isobel Neish. The mill dates from the eighteenth century, although the site was used for milling from at least the sixteenth century. Barry Mill came to the Trust largely as the result of the alertness and enthusiasm of local Trust members. It gives the Trust an important presence in the Dundee area and has augmented the representation of industrial archaeology. Both the mill itself and the mill lade are currently in the process of restoration.

Preston Mill in East Linton, East Lothian, goes back even further, for there is evidence to indicate a mill was in use there from the twelfth century. The mill was rebuilt in 1760, one of a chain of mills on the River Tyne which were needed to grind the grain, mainly oats, from the productive East Lothian farmers. Tenant farmers were normally thirled to the mill on the estate, which meant that they were obliged to have their grain ground there and to pay the miller in kind, with both a proportion of grain and help in maintaining the mill. The system was not popular with the tenant farmers – although the miller clearly did well out of it – but there were penalties for going elsewhere.

The mill buildings and equipment are distinctive, with a pantiled kiln and a huge iron wheel, about four metres in diameter and nearly a metre wide, probably cast at the Carron Ironworks near Falkirk. The whole process of milling is illustrated by this mill, which was in commercial operation until 1957. Associated with it are the millwrights James Meikle and his son Andrew, of nearby Phantassie. James Meikle was sent by Andrew Fletcher of Saltoun to the Netherlands to learn Dutch techniques of milling, which he introduced in East Lothian. Andrew Meikle's invention of a power-driven threshing machine in 1786 was an important contribution to the new agricultural technology. One of the leading civil engineers of the period, John Rennie, worked with Meikle for a time, before going on to design and build his own mills. In his later career he was involved with many of the most important engineering projects of the late eighteenth and early nineteenth centuries, including canal building and bridge and harbour works.

Preston Mill was presented to the Trust in 1950 by the trustees of the late Mr G B Gray. The buildings and machinery had deteriorated and had been further damaged by severe flooding in the summer of 1948. A partial repair was accomplished by local tradesmen. Then in 1966 the firm of Ranks Hovis MacDougall stepped in. The machinery was renewed and the mill restored to full working order. Ranks Hovis MacDougall came to the rescue again in 1972, when it was discovered that the mill wheel's wooden supports had rotted. In addition they have funded the recruitment of experienced staff to look after and run the mill. The Trust also owns the nearby Phantassie Doocot, which came to it in 1961, a gift from Mr William Hamilton of Phantassie Farm.

The miller's contribution to the agricultural community lay in the processing of the farmer's product. The smith's contribution was to the production itself. Since 1982 the Trust has owned a blacksmith's shop at Kippen, near Stirling, where it has been possible to maintain a working smiddy. It dates from the early eighteenth century, and the same family of smiths occupied the adjoining house and smiddy from 1721 to 1986.

The looms in the Weaver's Cottage, Kilbarchan.

In pre-industrial days the work of the smith was crucial to the community. As well as shoeing horses he made and repaired many small items, domestic as well as agricultural, and helped the farmer maintain his tools and implements in good order. Although it still contains traditional equipment the smiddy at Kippen is not a museum, but represents a nearly three-hundred-year continuum of smithing in the area. The gates for the National Trust for Scotland section at the Glasgow Garden Festival of 1988 were made in the Kippen smiddy, and are now at the Trust's Priorwood Garden in Melrose. The smiddy is only open to the public on advertised open days.

The most important home-based industry in Scotland's history has been handloom weaving, of wool and linen. The spinning of yarn and the weaving of woollen cloth went naturally with the keeping of sheep, and it has a very long history in Scotland. For centuries many Scottish households produced their own cloth, either for their own use or for sale. The spinning of flax and weaving of linen came later, but was well established by the sixteenth century, especially in the Tay and Clyde areas. In many rural households spinning went on in any 'spare' moment, and the humming of the spinning wheel was an almost constant accompaniment to other domestic activities. Although in earlier times the actual weaving was not necessarily carried out in the home, in the eighteenth century there were incentives to set up looms on domestic premises. There was an increasing demand for cloth, and with the mechanization of spinning the need for weavers grew – the development of power looms came later.

In Kilbarchan, a village near Paisley which was a major centre of weaving in the eighteenth and early nineteenth centuries, the Trust has a weaver's cottage where handloom weavers worked until 1940. The cottage was given to the Trust in 1954 by the family of the late Miss Christie. Built in 1723 by Andrew, John and Jenet Bryden and little altered since then, it is a characteristic cruck structure, supported by curved timbers at either end. As a typical vernacular building it is worthy of preservation in itself, but its lasting association with handloom weaving makes it doubly valuable.

The cottage combines as a restoration of a modest eighteenth-century home and as a museum of the tools and artefacts of the weaver. For at least two centuries weaving was the major occupation of the village. Like Paisley the Kilbarchan looms produced fine muslins and cambrics as well as wool and linen, and contributed to the production of shawls, for which the area became famous. The shawls, usually made from a silk and wool mixture, adapted designs that had their origins in Persia and Northern India. They reached the height of fashion in the first half of the nineteenth century. The handloom weavers of the area were hard hit when a combination of increasing mechanization and changing fashions dramatically lessened the demand for handwoven shawls, and many weavers either went to work in the factories or

The Weaver's Cottage, Kilbarchan.

emigrated. The Kilbarchan cottage is unusual in that handloom weaving continued there for so long.

Another reminder of Scotland's textile history is the weaver's workshop at the House of Dun in Angus. The weaving of linen damask on a handloom revives a traditional local industry. Textile production was one of the industries most dramatically affected by the Industrial Revolution, which followed close on the heels of agricultural improvement to speed up the process of change in Scotland. Mechanization of spinning and weaving was of particular advantage to the production of cotton, which used raw material imported to the Clyde mainly from America. The cotton industry was one of the factors contributing to the physical and economic growth of Glasgow, which by the early nineteenth century was a focal point of Scotland's industrial and commercial activity.

The factory-based Industrial Revolution stimulated textile production initially and then industries based on metallurgy and engineering. It dramatically affected the lives of those involved. Everyone in Scotland was touched by its consequences – the availability of new products, the general improvement of communications, the more affordable comforts and embellishments of the home. Few, also, could escape the less desirable affects – the exodus from country to city in search of employment, the too-rapid growth of urban areas and the consequent slums and health problems, the blighting effects of many kinds of industry on landscape and lifestyle, commented on by so many Victorians. But the conspicuous effects of progress and the increased production of commodities was at least as evident, and for most Victorians very important. Much of this was illustrated in people's homes, and most of the Trust's properties reveal the impact of Victorian attitudes and Victorian enterprise.

Amongst these is Brodick Castle, which for many decades received little attention. In the nineteenth century it was experiencing renewal. In 1810 the tenth Duke of Hamilton, owner of the estate, had married Susan Euphemia Beckford, daughter of William Beckford, a collector with eccentric and flamboyant tastes and author of the exotic novel *Vathek* (1786). Beckford inherited a fortune from his father, whose wealth derived from interests in the West Indies, and used it to indulge his passion for art and for travel. He housed his collection in Fonthill Abbey in Wiltshire, an extraordinary Gothic extravaganza designed for him by James Wyatt. On his death in 1844 his daughter inherited his wealth and his collection.

The year before her son, the Marquis of Douglas and Clydesdale, had married Princess Marie of Baden, and it was decided to refurbish Brodick as their home. The Beckford inheritance probably helped to finance this large-scale undertaking, and part of the collection was housed at Brodick, the remainder going to Hamilton Palace, the Duke's residence. The Duke approached the architect James

Brodick Castle and gardens.

Gillespie Graham, whose many buildings in Edinburgh included the Tolbooth Church and the later stages of the New Town, to take on the task of enlarging Brodick and bringing it up to date. Parts of the late thirteenth-, early fourteenth-century building survived, along with the battery that had been built by Cromwell's troops during their occupation in the mid-seventeenth century. Gillespie Graham more than doubled the size of Brodick, adding a new tower and an entrance, but blending old and new sympathetically.

Although the whole of the extensions planned by Gillespie Graham were not carried out the result of his work was a transformation that retained the uncompromising exterior of a medieval keep, but on the inside was a country house equipped for the lifestyle of Victorian aristocracy. The decoration was lavish, and the striking and eclectic nature of the Beckford material ensured that the interior had its own individuality, and this remains an essential part of the character of Brodick. Its modestly embellished outside stands in gardens that originate from the early eighteenth century, and against a dramatic mountain setting. Both are part of the Brodick heritage, for in 1958 Lady Jean Fforde donated to the Trust 6,600 acres of Arran countryside, including Goatfell, the island's highest mountain.

Like Culzean, Brodick has given the Trust a challenging opportunity to develop diverse aspects of conservation. These range from the maintenance of the house itself, and of the gardens, which include the

The Drawing Room, Brodick Castle.

The Dining Room at Brodick Castle, showing silver from the Beckford and Hamilton collections.

rhododendrons developed from cuttings from the garden created by the late Sir James Horlick on the island of Gigha, to the care of the estate which in 1980 became Scotland's first island country park. The garden is renowned for its prize-winning azaleas and rhododendrons. The Country Park is managed by the Trust and Cunninghame District Council in partnership, with financial support from the Countryside Commission for Scotland. A ranger service ensures that visitors are able to enjoy the countryside and its wildlife to the full. Current projects include a new Visitor Centre and the upgrading of educational facilities. The Trust's Education Department is particularly concerned with provision for schoolchildren, but almost every aspect of the Trust's work for and with the public involves education in the broadest sense. Education staff, visitor centres, publications, the ranger service, the supply of information in many different forms, are all part of the spectrum of educational facilities that the Trust provides.

Although its origins go back to Viking times Brodick can be included as one of Scotland's many monuments to Victorian enterprise. Another very different expression of enterprise was the garden created on the shores of Loch Ewe by a man of faith and vision. Osgood Mackenzie was the third son of the laird of Gairloch, and in 1862 his mother bought for him the barren, rocky peninsula *Am Ploc Ard* at the head of Loch Ewe.

Osgood Mackenzie, founder of Inverewe.

Three years later Mackenzie started planting, beginning with a windbreak as a shelter from the gales that swept across the Atlantic. Decades of devoted work turned an area of bare Torridonian sandstone into a luxuriant growth of trees, shrubs and plants.

This was the period when Scottish plant collectors were at their most adventurous, exploring and collecting in the Far East and the Americas, and Scottish gardeners were responding to new possibilities. Osgood Mackenzie's extraordinary achievement lay not just in the fact that he introduced exotic species and made the most of a high rainfall and the benign effects of the Gulf Stream, but that he created such inspired variety out of nothing. It was a combination of knowledge, inventiveness, experiment and sheer hard work – an army of workers had to carry in creel-loads of soil before planting was possible.

In 1952 Inverewe was given to the Trust by Osgood Mackenzie's daughter, Mrs Mairi Sawyer, who had taken on the care of the Garden after her father's death. Although an endowment came with the gift it was not sufficient for such a huge responsibility, and without the support of the Pilgrim Trust and a successful appeal it would have been a major risk for the Trust. The botanical and scientific value of the Garden is very great, but of course it attracts not just the specialist: many thousands of visitors wander through its fifty acres every year, and this fact in itself has posed a major challenge to the Trust, all the

Inverewe Garden.

Primula and blue mecanopsis at Inverewe.

greater as at the time Inverewe was acquired the Trust's experience with gardens was small.

The problem was to preserve the Garden and to retain as much of its character as possible, while making it accessible to visitors. To accomplish this meant the making of footpaths and the moving of plants, changes unavoidable if the Garden was to accommodate the public. The Trust had also to consider the fact that while most of Inverewe's visitors come in the summer, the garden is at its most spectacular during the springtime flowering of azaleas and rhododendrons. To ensure more colour in the busiest months a decision was made to introduce new shrubs and plants in the border between the gate lodge and the house. As with every Trust property conservation and public enjoyment are a matter of a fine and careful balance, and much of the Trust's effort goes into preserving that balance.

The Trust's commitment is both to environment, natural and historic, and to making properties both accessible and enjoyable, and Inverewe is a very good example of the success of this weighing of interests which can sometimes be seen to conflict. The need to provide for the public is strengthened as visitor numbers steadily increase, and this draws in every aspect of the services the Trust provides, from parking space to cups of tea (a new restaurant will be opening soon). Information about the Garden and its creator is readily available, through an exhibition, publications and the labelling of species.

There is also a commitment to the local community. The Trust is the major employer in the area, and the attraction of Inverewe brings a flood of visitors to Loch Ewe and Gairloch which benefits local hotels and services. The Trust has also contributed to the community in a number of practical ways, for example putting up a communal television aerial and helping to build a swimming pool.

There has been a sustaining of continuity at Inverewe, which bridges the period of Victorian bold resourcefulness and the upheavals and changed expectations brought by the twentieth century. A number of other Trust properties also take the story into the twentieth century, continuing the sequence of understanding which is an essential part of the Trust's undertaking.

CHAPTER EIGHT

Turning the Century

SCOTLAND entered the nineteenth century on the crest of the Industrial Revolution. Innovations in agriculture and industrial processes were backed by scientific enquiry and experiment, a prominent feature of the Enlightenment. Technological progress gained momentum, and by the time Queen Victoria came to the throne in 1837 there were few areas of life that were not being affected by the consequences. Although Scotland remained a primarily rural society both its population and the size of its cities were increasing rapidly. The Highlands had lost people through emigration abroad, often instigated and certainly encouraged by landlords wanting to change the use of the land, and through the drift to the cities.

The process of enclosure and the activities of landowners who rearranged, landscaped and planted their policies, usually for a combination of practical and aesthetic reasons, changed the face of the countryside. The contrast between hill and moor and fields neatly defined by dykes and hedges was clear. A network of roads had spread through areas where there had once been only rough paths. Bridges had been built, which made journeys easier and faster. On the coasts new harbourworks were constructed, and lighthouses went up to make the Scottish coastline safer for the increased shipping which was the inevitable result of expansion in industry and trade. Soon the railway would be cutting through the landscape, linking first the major cities and then reaching into the Highlands, which would never again seem quite so remote or divergent from the rest of Scotland.

Three small houses belonging to the Trust highlight some of the achievements of nineteenth-century Scotland. In the autumn of 1809 a nearly fourteen-year-old boy left the village of Ecclefechan in Annandale to walk to Edinburgh, where he was to become a student at the University. He had begun his education at the village school and Annan Grammar School, and later taught for a few years. By the middle of the century he was one of the best-known names in Victorian Britain. Thomas Carlyle was the son of a stonemason, and his father and uncle built the house in which he was born. The Arched House, built around 1791, is a pair of dwellings linked by an arch over a passageway.

Carlyle's upbringing was austerely religious, and he was destined for the ministry. But while in Edinburgh he was influenced by the legacy of the Enlightenment, and he turned instead to literature and history. He was particularly attracted by German literature, and wrote on Schiller and Goethe. By the 1830s he had established a reputation as a writer and lecturer of strong views and individual style. In 1835 he and his wife

Thomas Carlyle.

Jane Welsh Carlyle left Scotland for London, where he became a highly respected figure. He addressed himself to many social, political and historical issues, and was regarded as a man of exceptional learning and insight. In books such as *On Heroes and Hero Worship* (1841), *History of the French Revolution* (1837) and *Past and Present* (1843) he showed himself an uncompromising social and moral critic, and tireless in his expression of his at times authoritarian views. Although Carlyle spent half his life in London his thinking was shaped by his Scottish upbringing and education, and the religious and intellectual currents of the time.

Carlyle's family moved to another house in the village when he was three years old, but the Arched House remained the property of his uncle. In 1883, two years after Carlyle's death, the house was bought by Mrs Alexander Carlyle, the wife of one of his nephews (he had no children of his own). She began to collect material related to Carlyle, and opened the house to the public. In 1910 the house became the property of The Carlyle House Memorial Trust, which also owned the

Hugh Miller by D O Hill.

house in Cheyne Row, Chelsea, where Carlyle had lived with his wife. In 1935 the Trust took over the Arched House, and a year later the Cheyne Row house became the responsibility of the National Trust in England.

The Arched House is now arranged as a late eighteenth-century interior and also contains domestic and personal material associated with the Carlyles. It is a characteristic home of a modestly prosperous tradesman's family, with the kitchen as the most important room, a bedroom and a small room over half the arch. Amongst the contents of the house are items that belonged to Carlyle's parents, including the cradle that was used for Thomas, and material that was at Cheyne Row. The house is a reminder of the simplicity and determined values of Carlyle's background. His continued respect for these is underlined by his wish to be buried in Hoddam churchyard, a short distance from the house where he was born, rather than in Westminster Abbey.

Seven years after Carlyle's birth in Ecclefechan another of Scotland's most remarkable Victorian figures was born at the other end of the country. Hugh Miller, stonemason, geologist and writer, also came into the world in a small and modest dwelling, in the busy little port of Cromarty in Easter Ross. His father was a sea captain, who was drowned when Hugh was five years old. His mother was a Highlander, who after his father's death supported herself and her children by taking in needlework. As a child he keenly pursued the study of the natural world, which he preferred to book learning, and although a bright pupil at school he chose to become a stonemason rather than continue his education. His choice of trade gave him the opportunity to continue studying the rocks which were his main interest. His geological discoveries and writings, particularly the fossils he collected and described, brought him into contact with internationally-known geologists.

In the 1830s Miller changed direction and embarked on a career in banking, but he continued his involvement in geology. He was also a committed Presbyterian and took an active interest in church affairs, and wrote on a variety of subjects, although his best remembered books are those on geology, particularly *The Old Red Sandstone* (1840) and *The Testimony of the Rocks* (1857). In 1839 he moved to Edinburgh with his wife Lydia Fraser and their children. There he became editor of the evangelical newspaper *The Witness*, which strongly advocated the right of congregations to appoint their own ministers. This was one of the leading factors in the Disruption of the Church of Scotland in 1843, in which Miller played a prominent role. Miller responded very personally to the political, religious and scientific tensions of the times and was subject to depression: on Christmas Eve, 1856, he shot himself. His reputation as a geologist, and as a commentator on a great range of subjects, including folklore, church politics and social issues, was such that thousands turned out for his funeral.

Like Carlyle, Hugh Miller illustrates a distinctive current in Scottish society, which enabled those from modest and remote backgrounds to make a huge impact, in Miller's case without the benefit of much formal education. The cottage in Cromarty where he was born and grew up was built for Miller's great-grandfather in 1711, and is the only surviving house of the eighteenth-century town. It has been a museum since 1890, and in 1938 was donated to the Trust by Cromarty Town Council. It is now furnished as it might have been in the early nineteenth century, with two rooms given over to a display illustrating Miller's life and career, including a selection of fossils from his collection. The garden has recently been restored. The cottage is important as a reminder of seafaring traditions of Cromarty itself as well as of the origins of Hugh Miller.

When James Barrie was born in 1860 Hugh Miller had been dead for nearly four years but Thomas Carlyle was still very much alive and very productive. Barrie's contribution was to be rather different from that of the older men, but he would become just as well known. He made Kirriemuir, the town of his birth, well known as 'Thrums'. He began his literary career as a journalist on the *Nottinghamshire Journal*, and in 1885 went to London, where he soon established himself as a writer. As well as fiction, he was writing plays, the first of which was performed in 1891. He became internationally famous with his play *Peter Pan*, first performed in 1904, but many of his plays were popular, including *Quality Street*, *The Admirable Crichton*, *Dear Brutus* and *What Every Woman Knows*.

Kirriemuir was a rich source of inspiration, especially in Barrie's earlier writing. Like Carlyle and Miller, Barrie's origins were modest. David Barrie, his father, was a linen-weaver, who married Margaret Ogilvy, the daughter of a stonemason and a strong character. (It is interesting how the mason's trade links Carlyle, Miller and Barrie.) David Barrie worked at his loom in the house at 9 Brechin Road where James Matthew was born. Later he was able to move his loom to a rented loom shop, which allowed more space in the house for the family. By the time Barrie was born handloom weaving was being supplanted by the introduction of looms powered by steam. Factory weaving transformed the life of the town. Although in 1867 about 4000 people in Kirriemuir were involved in the linen industry, and in Forfarshire the town's linen production was second only to Dundee's, the coming of the power looms put many people out of work. David Barrie had to give up his life's occupation, and became a book-keeper in Forfar, and then a clerk back in Kirriemuir.

J M Barrie relied not only on his own experience of Kirriemuir for many of his stories but also on the experience of his mother. Margaret Ogilvy's memories and descriptions provided Barrie with a rich vein of material for fiction, and also for a book about her life, called *Margaret Ogilvy*. Thrums, the name of Barrie's fictional version of Kirriemuir, was a word meaning scraps of thread, often the ends of the warps. If his

J M Barrie's writing desk at his birthplace, Kirriemuir.

interpretation was rather sentimentalized, the house itself remains as solid evidence of his background. The house came to the Trust in 1937, donated by Duncan Elliot Alves of Bryn Bras Castle, Caernarvon, who soon after Barrie's death bought the house and the communal wash-house that stood in the yard. The wash-house, which the young Barrie had used as his first theatre, was also presented to the Trust. There had been some concern that the house would vanish entirely, for there was a suggestion that it might be removed stone by stone to the United States and re-erected as a museum. There was also a proposal to move the wash-house to Kensington Gardens, where Barrie used to meet the family of boys who were the first audience of stories about Peter Pan.

Barrie lived in the house of his birth, one of a group of houses called The Tenements, later known as Lilybank, until he was eight. The ground floor was taken up by the loom, with a kitchen and bedroom upstairs. Barrie was one of ten children, two of whom died very young. Margaret Ogilvy was ambitious for her children and encouraged James's education. He was an avid reader and decided at an early age that literature would be his profession. The writing desk he used in his London flat is now in the ground floor room, which his mother converted into a parlour after the removal of his father's loom. This room now contains a display of material related to Barrie's life, while the rooms upstairs have been restored to their nineteenth-century character. There is also a display in the wash-house, on the origins of *Peter Pan.*

From 1937 the house continued to be lived in by a friend of the Barrie family, so it was not until 1961 that the work of restoration began. The project involved providing accommodation for the Trust's representative, which was done by linking number 9 with number 11 next door. Although Barrie lived most of his life in London he returned often to Kirriemuir, and never severed his links with the community that had so powerfully fuelled his writing. He lived almost half his life in the twentieth century, yet he is just as rooted as Carlyle and Miller in the nineteenth century, and an equally important embodiment of Scottish achievement. The Trust's commitment to these modest homes of three giant figures of nineteenth-century Scotland is reflected in the fact that there is a special fund for maintaining them.

Between them Carlyle, Miller and Barrie span nearly a century and a half. When Barrie died in 1937⸍ the issues that preoccupied the Victorians had given way to the events and concerns that followed in the wake of a world war of unforeseeable dimensions. But the years before the First World War were for some the zenith of a lifestyle that would soon disappear, and they also saw some of the most distinguished achievements in design and architecture since the days of the Adams. The Trust has properties which illustrate both these aspects of late Victorian and Edwardian Scotland.

In 1877 Kellie Castle had been largely untended for nearly half a century. On the death of the childless tenth Earl of Kellie in 1829 the contents were sold up, and the inheritor, John Erskine, Earl of Mar, had no need of the castle as a residence. But in 1877 it took on a new lease of life, when it was discovered and adopted by the Lorimer family. James Lorimer, Professor of Public and International Law at the University of Edinburgh, regularly holidayed in Fife with his family – the coming of the railways had made seaside and country holidays a possibility for many families. It was while the Lorimers were staying in Pittenweem that they came upon the neglected Kellie Castle. There were gaping holes in the roof, the windows were broken, the ceilings were sagging, rooks, owls and swallows were nesting inside and out, and the garden was a wilderness. The following year, having negotiated a lease with the Earl of Mar, the Lorimer family moved in. Between them landlord and tenants had made the house habitable, and the Lorimers

The nursery at Kellie Castle.

would continue to make such improvements as they could afford in the years they were there.

For the next sixty years members of the Lorimer family spent their summers at Kellie Castle. And they were rather a remarkable family. Professor Lorimer married Hannah Stoddart, of musical background, and their six children were all distinctively talented. The three most closely associated with Kellie were John Lorimer the painter, Robert Lorimer the celebrated architect, and Louise Lorimer, one of the first woman students at Edinburgh University. Louise tackled the garden. John, who achieved youthful fame as a portrait painter, spent his summers at Kellie until his death in 1937 at the age of eighty. But the imprint of Kellie was perhaps most marked on Robert Lorimer, whose architecture expresses an understanding of Scottish vernacular style influenced by his early experience of rescuing Kellie Castle.

After the death of John Lorimer the next generation of Lorimers took on the mantle of Kellie. Hew Lorimer, son of Robert, and his wife Mary McLeod Wylie, continued to rent Kellie until in 1948 they decided to buy it. With the help of grants from the Historic Buildings Council for

Scotland the Lorimers set about the major repairs that were needed. But they did much more than repair the fabric of the building. Mary Lorimer, a versatile artist, set about the task of redecorating and refurbishing the interior with unrivalled sensitivity and dedication. Not only did she design and choose colour schemes, she carried out much of the work with her own hands, for she was a skilled painter, embroiderer and upholsterer. Kellie's distinctive character owes much to her commitment, and to the fact that it has been little tampered with structurally. It escaped eighteenth- and nineteenth-century extension, and each generation of the Lorimers has been anxious to enhance rather than transform the building. Its simple, solid, unpretentious aspect remains undisturbed.

In 1970 Kellie Castle and most of its contents were acquired by the Trust. The purchase was made possible by a grant from the Secretary of State for Scotland through the National Land Fund and by further assistance from the Pilgrim Trust and an anonymous source. Money to purchase the contents also came from the National Land Fund. As well as the items that were purchased Kellie also still contains material loaned by Hew Lorimer. But, as always, the Trust could not have taken on the responsibility of Kellie without an endowment to provide for its maintenance. The bulk of this came from the same anonymous donor who contributed to the purchase price.

The most dramatic phase of the restoration of Kellie came when the fine plaster ceiling of the Great Hall was found to be cracking. With help from government agencies an ambitious rescue operation was put in hand. The floor above was removed and steel beams were inserted to take the weight off the ceiling. With the pressure on the plasterwork successfully relieved it was possible to reinstate the floor, with the rooms above and below safely preserved.

The significance of Kellie is highlighted by travelling a short distance to the west, to a house built in 1906 for Frederick Bower Sharp, the son of a highly successful jute merchant. Jute had supplanted linen as Dundee's major industry, and in the 1860s production of jute cloth from hemp imported from Bengal expanded enormously. The successful preparation of jute depended on Dundee's other major occupation, whaling, for whale oil was an essential ingredient in the process. For a short time Dundee dominated the world production of jute. This was the foundation of the fortune which John Sharp left to his children, and it provides a window on another aspect of Victorian Scotland, although the house that is its monument was built in Edwardian times.

The connection with Kellie comes through Robert Lorimer, for he was the architect of Hill of Tarvit, the house for Frederick Sharp. Frederick was the youngest son of four, and although he spent some years with the family business his main involvement was in finance. He invested in the expanding railways and became a director of the

Hill of Tarvit.

Caledonian Railway, and was on the board of the London-Midland-Scottish. By 1904 he was well established, a wealthy and respected man of business with a wife, Beatrice, and a son. He had built up an interesting collection of furniture, decorative art and pictures and felt it was time to think of an appropriate space for them, his family and his lifestyle. His first step was to buy a seventeenth-century house near Cupar, called Wemyss Hall, which was possibly the work of the architect William Bruce. Nearby was Scotstarvit Tower, an older tower house which had fallen into disrepair.

Robert Lorimer was by 1904 an architect of considerable reputation, as a designer of both private houses and public buildings. He had a keen understanding of old houses, encouraged by the years at Kellie. The challenge of Hill of Tarvit was not just to work with an existing structure, but to create spaces that would be sympathetic to Sharp's collection, and to the Fife countryside. In the new part of the house, built in front of the two wings that had been added in Victorian times, he provided a splendid but comfortable hall which accommodated Sharp's sixteenth-century Flemish tapestries, a number of paintings, mainly portraits, and his collection of Chinese bronzes and porcelain. The room's oak panelling gives a pleasant impression of warmth and security. The plaster ceiling is decorated with a motif of vines that echoes one of the ceilings at Kellie. The drawing room, library and dining room each have a character of their own, complementing and enhancing the pictures and furnishings.

Life at Hill of Tarvit exemplified a facet of Edwardian Scotland often characterized as the lull before the storm of the First World War. It was a life of comfort and leisure, which in the case of the Sharp family survived the economic and practical tribulations of the War. Frederick Sharp's business commitments left him ample time for the pursuits of a country gentleman. There was a garden to enjoy, also designed by Lorimer, and tennis and golf were popular. Friends were entertained. When Sharp died in 1932 his son Hugh continued a wide range of business and financial involvements, but he too had time for other interests. He led an active life, sailing round the Scottish coasts in his yacht, and hunting, shooting and skiing. But Hugh Sharp was tragically killed in the Castlecary rail disaster in 1937, which left 179 injured and thirty-five dead. He was on his way to visit his fiancée, Mabel Hogarth, daughter of a Cardross shipping family, to whom he was to be married six days later.

Beatrice Sharp and her daughter Elizabeth continued to live at Hill of Tarvit, both devoting themselves to working in the community and by choice leading a life very different from the ample existence of earlier days. Mrs Sharp died in 1946, and her daughter two years later, of cancer. It seems a sad and quiet end to the Sharps of Hill of Tarvit, but the future of the house they created was assured. With the help of Lord Grimond, a family friend with his own connections with the Dundee jute industry and at that time Secretary of the National Trust for Scotland, Elizabeth Sharp had arranged for Hill of Tarvit, its collections and an endowment to go to the Trust. Initially only the ground floor was opened to the public, as part of the house was used by the Marie Curie Foundation as a nursing home until 1977, when their improved fortunes enabled them to make use of more appropriate premises. By that time the Trust was in a position to undertake more radical work on the house. More rooms were opened, while the Victorian part of the house was converted into flats for letting. More recently the Trust has worked on the restoration of the Edwardian kitchen, butler's pantry and bathroom. An important contribution to the refurbishment of Hill of Tarvit came from the volunteer textile restoration team based at the house. The team consists of Trust members who carry out invaluable textile restoration for properties all over Scotland.

The Trust has maintained this remarkable house as an illustration both of a way of life and of the particular tastes and energies of the Sharp family. Features such as the Edwardian kitchen and bathroom show the domestic organization of a substantial country house, the running of which was dependent on a hierarchy of servants and a careful definition of responsibilities. The design of Victorian and Edwardian homes reflected the importance of the relationship between a family and its servants, a way of life and the work behind the scenes that maintained it. Hill of Tarvit gives the visitor the opportunity to explore an Edwardian home, and also to enjoy the paintings and objects that were the direct result of John and Frederick Sharp's industrial and business success.

Success of a different kind is memorialized in a house designed by Robert Lorimer's contemporary, Charles Rennie Mackintosh. In 1902 the Glasgow publisher Walter Blackie commissioned Mackintosh to design a house for him on a hill in Helensburgh, overlooking the Firth of Clyde. The Hill House was completed in 1904, the same year Frederick Sharp took his first step towards Hill of Tarvit. Mackintosh was thirty-four years old when he started work on The Hill House and had already made a considerable impact with his designs, of interiors and furniture as well as buildings. He had achieved particular distinction with his design for the Glasgow School of Art, where he himself had been a student, attending evening classes while apprenticed to the firm of John Hutchison. He had also designed several of the Cranston Tea Rooms and Windyhill, a house for William Davidson in Kilmacolm.

Blackie had distinct views on what he wanted, and had taken an interest in the Glasgow Style which Mackintosh and his associates had developed. Blackie wanted an unfussy house which would suit his business and family needs, and would reflect the traditions of vernacular Scottish building rather than imitate imported architectural styles. His requirements coincided with Mackintosh's views on suiting style to environment and function. The result was a bold and modern design, with a plain exterior strongly suggestive of Scottish tradition and an interior gracefully adapted to modern life. Mackintosh worked from the inside out, concentrating first on the interior space before designing its outer frame.

The house was designed for a comfortable and elegant way of life, appropriate for a confidently successful man and his family. Perhaps more precisely than Hill of Tarvit it illustrates the relationship between business (a male preserve) and family life, and between domestic living and the infrastructure that sustained it. The library, where Blackie could see his clients, was separate from the living areas, the children's nursery and schoolroom were at a distance from the business part of the house, and the service area – kitchen, pantries, laundry and so on – were in a separate wing. Mackintosh preferred to design the whole of an interior, including the fittings and furniture, but in the case of The Hill House Blackie wanted some space suitable for his existing furniture, and also wanted to avoid unnecessary expense. Mackintosh totally designed only four rooms, the hall, library, drawing room and main bedroom, but the overall decorative scheme he developed blended with Walter Blackie's furniture and also provided continuity.

In 1953 the house was sold to T Campbell Lawson, who was anxious to preserve its character. When he came to sell it nineteen years later his priority was to ensure the future of the house and its furniture. It was bought by the Royal Incorporation of Architects of Scotland, who established a trust to maintain the house as a lived-in residence. The

The Hall, the Hill House.

The White Bedroom, the Hill House.

service wing was converted into flats. A number of bodies, including the Landmark Trust, Strathclyde Regional Council, Dumbarton District Council and the William Robertson Charitable Trust contributed grants. In May 1982 the acceptance of the house and contents by the National Trust for Scotland was made possible by a generous contribution from the National Heritage Memorial Fund. Since then the Trust has worked towards restoring the house as nearly as possible to its original state. With the help of the Blackie family the Trust has been able to recreate their early twentieth-century home while at the same time illustrating Mackintosh's achievement. Loans and donations from the Blackie family and other individuals and organizations have helped to make this possible.

Charles Rennie Mackintosh never achieved in his lifetime the recognition in Britain that was awarded him on the Continent, where he was seen as a pioneer of new and distinctive styles and was very influential. In The Hill House and Hill of Tarvit the Trust has in its care examples of Scotland's two most significant early twentieth-century architects, one an adventurous innovator, the other an inventive interpreter, and incomparable memorials to the Edwardian period and to Scottish achievement in two of her major cities. But of course they represent the life of a minority and the achievement of the exceptional. Another of the Trust's properties, an ordinary Glasgow home dating from almost the same period, provides a balance.

In 1975 the actress Anna Davidson accompanied her uncle to 145 Buccleuch Street in Glasgow, where he was collecting some chairs left to him in the will of its late owner. She found an interior that had changed little since its occupation in 1911 by the family that remained there for over sixty years, and contents that provided an extraordinary personal and social record of this time. She was so intrigued by what she found that she bought the flat and kept it as close as possible to the way she found it. When she had to leave seven years later she sold it to the Trust, anxious that its unique documentation should be in safe hands.

Glasgow in the nineteenth century had changed perhaps more than any other Scottish city. Where other cities grew at the margins Glasgow experienced a major transformation at its centre, with the result that at first sight it now appears to be without the historic layers that are so much present in Edinburgh. It was the speed of development that was partly the reason for this – in the middle of the nineteenth century Glasgow was doubling its population in ten years. The city was a magnet, for it was at the heart of the area of Scotland's most vigorous industrial activity, with a constant need for labour. The cotton industry was supplanted by steel and industries dependent on steel, the chief of which was shipbuilding. The need of the steel industry for coal stimulated the Lanarkshire coalmines. Although less important, the textile industry continued, and the splendidly ornate Templeton's carpet factory, a building based on the Doge's Palace in Venice, is a monument not just to the Glasgow textile industry but to how Glasgow's manufacturers saw themselves.

Glasgow is unusual amongst industrial cities in that most of the industry itself lay on the fringes of the city. Those who worked in the mines, the shipyards and the factories tended to live in the city, and travel out to their places of work. As well as heavy industry there were all the associated businesses and service industries offering employment. To accommodate this huge concentration of people Glasgow built upwards, and the tenement was the characteristic dwelling. In some areas large numbers of people were crammed into one- and two-room flats, and although attempts were made to control overcrowding this was often difficult. But there were also tenements that offered more spacious accommodation for a growing lower-middle class, as well as the elegant terraces that went up in the Georgian period to house those who benefited most from Glasgow's success.

Glasgow expanded westward in the late eighteenth and early nineteenth centuries, and that momentum continued. In the 1820s the Blythswood estate, next to Sauchiehall Street, was laid out in a grid pattern for new terraces, and the result was Blythswood Square and the streets around it, a fashionable suburb. The 1840s saw tenements going up to the north again, in Hill Street and Renfrew Street, and gradually the development expanded. Another flurry of building activity took place in the 1890s, which included, as well as more tenements on Buccleuch Street, Mackintosh's School of Art. Further away from the centre grander terraces went up, and spacious villas for the well-off.

The Parlour, the Tenement House, Glasgow.

The tenement at 145 Buccleuch Street was completed in 1892, built by James Ferguson of the building firm Ferguson and Anderson. It was bought by Dougald McCorkindale, a coalmaster. In 1911 Mrs Toward, a widowed dressmaker whose husband, a salesman in metals, had died in 1889, moved in, with her twenty-five-year-old daughter Agnes. Agnes Toward had grown up and gone to school in the area, while she and her mother had lived at a number of addresses and Mrs Toward had struggled to run a draper's business. In Buccleuch Street she continued her dressmaking and also took in lodgers to help make ends meet. In 1914 Agnes joined the shipping firm of Prentice, Service and Henderson in Hope Street, not far away, and was a shorthand typist with them until she retired at the age of seventy-three.

The consistency of her working life was echoed in her domestic circumstances. She never married, and made few changes in her home – the only major innovation was the installation of electricity in 1960. She usually went on holiday to the same place, Largs, and enjoyed the same leisure activities, especially dancing and theatre-going. And she discarded very little. The house contains the accumulated evidence of over half a century of Agnes Toward's life, and is also a microcosm of Glasgow tenement life in the early part of the century. The renewal work undertaken by the Trust has concentrated on preserving the house's early twentieth-century character. Wallpapers have been carefully matched, and the original gas lighting has been reinstated: the first

The kitchen range in the Tenement House.

sensation experienced by the visitor is the faint smell and hiss of the gas lighting.

The house's four rooms, which include a bathroom, still at that time an uncommon amenity except in recent buildings, are small but pleasantly proportioned. Both the parlour and the kitchen have box beds, which may have been occupied by Agnes and her mother while the lodger had the bedroom. The furniture is functional, with the kitchen retaining a range, fed with coal from the bunker opposite, which even before the First World War did not represent the height of kitchen technology. Agnes Toward made no renovations and accumulated few of the commodities that became increasingly available as the century wore on, but a sense of comfort and agreeableness remain. It must have been a highly desirable residence for two not very well-off women before the First World War.

The Kitchen, the Tenement House.

The Toward flat is in a tenement building which is, of course, still occupied by other families, and the Trust's provision for visitors has had to adapt to these circumstances. It has been able to purchase three other flats in the building, which has allowed space for a visitor reception area and premises for its representative. The Tenement House (like the Georgian House) is staffed by volunteer guides; it is another example of the invaluable contribution of volunteers to the Trust's work.

The Tenement House is a remarkable encapsulation of a living environment that has survived without the layers of change and renewal that are customary. This is part of what makes it almost unique amongst Trust properties. Its particular value lies in the dual preservation of an aspect of life in the past that does not often survive, and of an environment half a century old that has not had to be reconstructed. The evidence of ordinary lives is least often preserved, because it is most vulnerable to change and its value in the broad perspectives of history tends to be overlooked. The Tenement House displays the material fabric of one of these ordinary lives, backed up by the documentary evidence preserved by Agnes Toward herself. Its intimate scale puts the visitor closely in touch with life in the recent past, which is still near enough to many people's experience for them to feel at home there.

CHAPTER NINE

Islands and Other Communities

SCOTLAND'S islands contribute a distinctive quality to the nation's character and heritage. Island communities have over the centuries represented particular currents of determined survival, and maintained traditions that are often more likely to be eroded on the mainland. The inevitable separateness of Scotland's islands has been both a problem, sometimes of insurmountable proportions, and a strength. If the Trust had no islands in its care it would be without an essential feature of Scotland's past and present. In fact it has several, ranging from uninhabited loch-bound fragments of land to the islands of Fair Isle and St Kilda with their own very distinctive histories. Islands have constituted some of the Trust's biggest tests, but also demonstrate the extent and diversity of its successes.

Islands are communities determined by geography, but there are many other factors that shape a community, and the Trust's properties reflect these in a number of ways. Whether they highlight a particular occupation, as the weaver's cottage at Kilbarchan does, or illustrate the relations between families and the fortunes of Scotland, as do so many of the great houses, or show the changing patterns of landscape and land use, these properties bring into focus both a close-up on the past and the actions of time. They are tangible evidence not only of 'history' but of continuity, for whatever changes there have been the properties remain in their original context. Vital in maintaining the links between property and community are the Trust's representatives, whose work embraces far more than the properties in their charge. Their participation in community life fosters a mutually supportive relationship.

Historically, many of the Trust's properties have been both the source of change, and the reflection of change. Now, of course, the Trust's main task is often to preserve and protect what is vulnerable because it is no longer viable. But in other cases the Trust is making a contribution towards continuing viability. The Little Houses Improvement Scheme is an outstanding example of this, as it gives new life to old buildings without damaging their historic nature. Culross survives both as an historic burgh illustrating aspects of Scotland's seventeenth-century economic success, and as a thriving twentieth-century community. An important feature of the scheme is that the Trust prefers to sell or let to those who are working in the community. Culross and Dunkeld are perhaps the most conspicuous and most dramatic examples of the Trust's community involvement through the Little Houses Improvement Scheme, but are only two of several.

The scheme has made its mark particularly in Fife, with the

restoration of houses in Crail, Dysart, Pittenweem, Tayport, Ceres and St Monans in addition to the major initiative in Culross. But all over Scotland are little houses which have benefited, in the Borders, in Perthshire (particularly Dunkeld) and Inverness, in the west of Scotland, in Angus and Aberdeenshire. One restoration involved the community in rather an unusual way. When Peter Clark took on Powrie Castle in Dundee as a restoring purchaser he encountered problems with local vandals. In a persuasive encounter with them he suggested that instead of dismantling his efforts they put their energies to more creative use, and successfully enlisted their help in the restoration work.

There are other kinds of involvement which are deliberately inconspicuous. The island of Canna, one of the Small Isles of the Inner Hebrides, was the gift to the Trust in 1981 of Dr John Lorne Campbell. Dr Campbell and his wife Margaret Fay Shaw, who live in Canna House on the island, are Gaelic scholars and musicians committed to the sustaining of Gaelic culture. Dr Campbell is also keen to protect natural habitats. Canna, five miles long and a mile wide, and the adjoining smaller island of Sanday have been designated a Site of Special Scientific Interest by the Nature Conservancy Council. Canna's bird population is of particular interest: 157 species have been recorded, of which seventy-one have bred on the island. There are breeding colonies of puffins, razorbills, guillemots, black guillemots, fulmars, kittiwakes and manx shearwaters. Dr Campbell has been responsible for regenerating the island's woodland, which has encouraged the number of woodland species now found on Canna.

The significance of Canna lies not just in the fact that it is a protected environment for wildlife, but that this goes hand in hand with human habitation and livelihood. Evidence suggests that Canna was inhabited in the Stone Age, and there are traces of early Christian, Viking and Celtic settlements. In the Middle Ages it was part of the endowment of the Benedictine Monastery founded on Iona by Queen Margaret in 1074, and then became Macdonald of Clanranald territory.

Dr Campbell acquired the island in 1938. In 1981 came his gift of the island itself, which was backed by a grant from the National Heritage Memorial Fund. As Canna's landlord the Trust is committed not only to protection, but to regeneration. Canna's population dwindled, but is now growing again. It is hoped that as it demonstrates the viability of a traditional crofting community more people will be attracted to the island. Hill sheep-farming is the basis of the economy, with some cattle, and crops are grown to provide winter feed. Lobster fishing is also viable, and the Trust is involved in trying out the possibilities of oyster farming. The Trust's responsibility is to a living community, an environment where human activity is entirely compatible with flourishing wildlife. Dr Campbell continues in Canna, and his long-established understanding of both the community and the countryside support the Trust's commitment.

Far to the north and east, midway between Orkney and Shetland, lies the Trust's northernmost property, an island even smaller than Canna. Fair Isle came to the Trust in 1954. It had been bought after the Second World War from the Sumburgh estate in mainland Shetland by George Waterston the ornithologist, who with Ian Pitman recognized its unique value for the observation and recording of migratory birds. Their plans for Fair Isle evolved in a German prisoner-of-war camp. The island offers an ideal resting place for birds on the wing, and has a greater variety of bird migrants than all the rest of Scotland. It had long attracted the interest of naturalists, but it was not until George Waterston established an observatory there that systematic record-keeping and analysis became possible. Waterston set about converting buildings abandoned by the Navy, who had been in occupation during the War, to provide working space and accommodation for visiting scientists.

Archaeological findings on Fair Isle go back to the Iron Age. In the twelfth century the island was under Viking rule, and its Viking past is reflected in many of the place-names. The population has fluctuated considerably: in the mid-nineteenth century there were 380 people on Fair Isle, gaining a livelihood by fishing and crofting. By the middle of the twentieth there were less than fifty, a decline that had accelerated in the preceding decades. This depletion reflected the pattern in many of the remoter parts of Scotland. The bird observatory was a great success, but, like many of the birds themselves, its visitors were temporary and could contribute little to the regeneration of the island's population. And the observatory required resources for its continued success. For these reasons George Waterston turned to the Trust. Both the observatory and Fair Isle needed a commitment of larger proportions.

In some respects Fair Isle's past provides encouragement for the future. The sea was one source of livelihood. The islanders were expert fishermen, and had devised their own distinctive type of boat, the yoal, which was well-suited to negotiate the uncertainties of Fair Isle's rocky coast. They also benefited from being on a trade route, busy enough to warrant the construction towards the end of the nineteenth century of lighthouses at the north and south ends of the island. The islanders would trade with passing ships, exchanging fresh food – fish, eggs, vegetables – for commodities they could not produce themselves. They also traded the products of their knitting needles. The origins of the distinctive Fair Isle knitting style are not precisely known, but the skill and imagination that has gone into developing endless variations in colour and detail are self-evident. Knitting was the natural corollary of sheep-farming, an important aspect of Fair Isle crofting. Both spinning the yarn and knitting it up were activities that could be carried on in the home in the midst of other work.

Barley and oats were grown on the island and in the nineteenth century the grain was ground in mills powered by the Burn of Gilsetter which runs down to the east coast. The mills have not been used since the First World War, but there are plans to restore one of them. It is clear that in the nineteenth century there was a flourishing community on Fair Isle, with an economy that went beyond subsistence, although the landlords benefited from this more than the tenants. A school was founded in 1730, and Fair Isle children still receive all their primary schooling on the island.

When the Trust acquired Fair Isle in 1954 it seemed a neglected and unpromising crofting community. Communications were poor – the mail boat the *Good Shepherd* called once a week when the weather allowed. With talk of evacuation in the air Fair Isle was a risky proposition for the Trust, for as landlord it would be liable to pay compensation to those who chose to leave. And the future was precarious. Aside from crofting there was virtually no employment. Fishing was no longer on a commercial basis, and there were few outlets for knitted goods. Major trade routes had long since bypassed Fair Isle. It was clear that a major and collaborative effort would be required to regenerate the island.

The Trust's commitment was itself a reassurance, and with the co-operation of a number of bodies, Zetland County Council, the Highlands and Islands Advisory Council, the Scottish Council (Development and Industry) and others, a scheme was devised. The first step was to improve communications. The Post Office agreed to increase the sailings of the *Good Shepherd* and Zetland County Council took on the construction of a new pier, to which the Trust contributed £1000. It was completed in 1958. The Trust initiated a modernization programme for the croft houses, which was helped by various groups of volunteers. Looms were introduced and training in weaving, and there was help in marketing both woven and knitted goods. Now Fair Isle Crafts is a flourishing co-operative, producing both hand- and machine-knitted garments. Advice was available on crofting techniques, and there has been careful encouragement of new settlers on the island.

Gradually the process of change took effect. In 1982 a wind-driven generator was installed which provides electricity twenty-four hours a day for the sixty-nine islanders. The airstrip, constructed in the Second World War and then abandoned, was enlarged in the 1970s and is now used by Loganair, which runs scheduled flights. A new slipway for the *Good Shepherd IV*, the successor of the earlier mail boats, provides vital protection from winter storms. There are plans to construct a breakwater at North Haven as a further bulwark against the weather. In 1969 a new building was put up for the observatory, which continues as a centre for data collection and for special studies on migration, ecology and genetics. All the island's sea cliffs have been designated Sites of Special Scientific Interest by the Nature Conservancy Council. Acknowledgement for this work came in 1986 with the award of the

Good Shepherd IV at the jetty, Fair Isle.

Fair Isle.

Council of Europe Diploma in recognition of Fair Isle's achievement in working in harmony with the environment. This compatibility of interests is vital. Fair Isle is a community shared by the whole of the island's population, not just the human inhabitants, and its survival rests on mutual dependence. Again, the Trust's responsibility has been a matter of getting the balance right.

In Fair Isle as in Canna the Trust took on a commitment not just to maintaining but to revitalizing human habitation. With St Kilda the challenge was rather different, for when the Trust acquired that most distant (apart from Rockall) of Britain's islands there was no one living on it. St Kilda came to the Trust in 1957. In 1931, a year after St Kilda had been evacuated at the islanders' request, it had been bought from Sir Reginald MacLeod of MacLeod by the fifth Marquess of Bute. He acquired a group of dramatically craggy islands, the home of thousands of seabirds. That St Kilda should have sustained a human population at all is something that has intrigued people for centuries. The four islands and five towering rock stacks are 110 miles west of the Scottish

Puffins on St Kilda.

Boreray, St Kilda.

mainland. The nearest neighbour is North Uist, forty odd miles away. The islands themselves offered little opportunity for crofting beyond using the good grazing for keeping animals. There was very little cultivation, with low yields of barley and oats, and later potatoes. Curiously, there was not much interest in fishing, and the main sources of food were seabirds and their eggs.

With extraordinary skill and agility, in managing small boats off the rocky coast and in scaling cliffs, birds were trapped and eggs were collected. Gannets, fulmars and puffins were the main prizes. Food and materials were stored in stone cleits roofed with turf, which are still scattered over the main islands.

The islands themselves came into being as a result of volcanic action, and have since been shaped by millions of years of erosion from sea, rain and ice. The outstanding features of the group are the rock stacks and sheer cliff walls, some well over 300 metres high. The islands have produced their own distinctive animal and plant life, with not only an extraordinary bird population but island forms of the wren and the fieldmouse as well as Soay sheep, which may be related to the earliest domesticated sheep brought to Britain in about 5000 BC.

It is believed that the earliest human settlement of St Kilda occurred some time in the second millennium BC, but it is impossible to establish who the first settlers were. Numerous bronze age remains survive, cairns, burial cists and the boat graves – boat-shaped arrangements of stones – which are peculiar to the islands. Some time between the first and third centuries AD there seems to have been a new settlement, in Village Bay on Hirta, the largest island. A souterrain, or earth house, dating from that period has been thoroughly excavated and finds have included potsherds, quernstones, stone lamps, hammerstones, and numerous animal bones. Many of these objects are now in the National Museums of Scotland. A second settlement at Gleann Mor probably flourished between about the sixth and the fourteenth centuries. There was some Viking influence on the island though not sufficient evidence to suggest that there was any longterm settlement – most of the place names are Gaelic rather than Norse. Early Christian influence is also apparent, but again little is known of its effect or its extent.

In 1697 St Kilda was visited by Martin Martin, who published an account of the community there. He described a society that was primitive, apparently contented, but which paid little attention to Christian teaching. An attempt to do something about the latter was made in 1705, when a missionary was sent to St Kilda by the Society for the Propagation of Christian Knowledge. Gradually an awareness of St Kilda grew and in the nineteenth century it had a certain attraction for tourists. Wealthy trippers visited St Kilda, some more out of curiosity to see what was regarded by many as a strange, anachronistic tribe than out of real interest in the geology, natural history or society of the islands.

Previous contact with the outside world had mainly consisted of the

Village Bay, Hirta, St Kilda's largest island, with Soay sheep in the foreground.

annual visit from the MacLeod tacksman to collect the rent. With the arrival of tourist ships the St Kildans had the opportunity to sell tweeds, knitwear and sealskins, and this exposure to a money economy inevitably had its effect on the traditional way of life. Gradually there was less reliance on the old skills and more on contacts with the mainland. Although this contact brought an awareness of the islands' needs and some benefits, such as the new cottages financed by MacLeod of MacLeod, the undermining of tradition could not be reversed, and it was perhaps inevitable that the St Kildans would eventually be forced to abandon Village Bay and seek another life elsewhere.

Scientific interest in the islands remained, and it was this that motivated the Marquess of Bute's purchase of the islands. When they came to the Trust they were leased to the Nature Conservancy Council; they in turn have leased a part of Hirta to the Ministry of Defence which maintains a missile-tracking station there. The Army presence has been an asset, providing telecommunications and medical services, and assisting with the transport of materials used in the work of conservation, although it also created the Trust's first major problem in St Kilda. The Army planned to make use of the stone from the dilapidated Village Bay cottages to provide the bottoming for a new road. If the Trust had not been able to persuade them otherwise conservation of the village would have been impossible: the vital materials would have disappeared.

Conservation has been the Trust's main objective. The initial aim has been to preserve the buildings of Village Bay, not for habitation but as a museum of St Kilda life. To accomplish this the Trust in 1958 instituted a programme of summer working parties. Every year groups of volunteers have worked hard at clearance and restoration. Cottages have been restored, and every summer Village Bay comes to life again as a working community. The nature of the work has changed since the days of permanent habitation, but it is both demanding and rewarding, and simply being on St Kilda is a unique experience. In 1986 St Kilda became UNESCO's first World Heritage Site in the United Kingdom, a tribute to the work that had been done and an encouragement for the future. The St Kilda working parties continue to be a major event in the Trust's year.

The preservation of these distinctive aspects of human and natural history and culture on Scotland's geographical edge – and for much of their history on the edge of Scotland's consciousness – is important in itself. But the Trust has also brought these islands closer to the public. Through the initiative of the Robertson family the Trust tradition of ship cruising started with the *Lady Killarney* in the 1950s. On 21 September 1961 the British India Steam Navigation Company's *Dunera* left the Firth of Clyde for the first of the major island cruises. The *Dunera* steamed 1500 miles in five days, visiting Inverewe, St Kilda, Lerwick and Fair Isle, and returning to the Firth of Forth. Amongst the passengers – the *Dunera* could accommodate 150 in cabins and another 600 in dormitories – were lecturers on ornithology, gardening, archaeology, geology and history. The following year there were two cruises, the first leaving from South Queensferry for Fair Isle, Foula, St Kilda, Inverewe, Stornoway, Brodick and Greenock, the second making the trip in reverse order. These early cruises, the result of a pioneering vision and a spirit of adventure, were so successful there was no question but that they should continue. They offered, and continue to offer, an unrivalled opportunity to explore some of the less accessible parts of Scotland, in the company of experts in a number of different fields. Cruises in recent years have taken visitors further afield, to Scandinavia and the Baltic, a reminder of Scotland's environmental and centuries-old historical links with northern Europe.

The cruises have brought benefits to the Trust of a very tangible kind, in particular the North American connection. This had been fostered by Culzean and the Eisenhower link and by the very real American interest in the work of the Trust. In 1965, thanks to the initiative of John Ward Melville who had participated enthusiastically in the early cruises, the Scottish-American Heritage Inc, later renamed Scottish Heritage (USA) Inc, was set up. Its objective was to 'recognize and enhance the original bonds of ancestral and national character among the peoples of Scotland and North America'.

The cruise ship Black Prince *visiting St Kilda.*

The organization has been supportive of the Trust in many valuable ways and there has been a mutually beneficial exchange of ideas and expertise. A striking example of this is centred on the School of Horticulture at Threave, founded by the Trust in 1960 to make the best use of the donation of the Threave estate by Major Alan Gordon. Threave is linked with Longwood Gardens, Pennsylvania, in a two-way exchange programme financed by SHUSA. Each year a student sponsored from Longwood comes to Threave and a Threave student goes to Longwood. Thus Threave demonstrates both the Trust's commitment to training, and the flourishing and creative relationship with the United States. Gardeners trained at Threave can be found in horticultural jobs all over the world. SHUSA has funded other aspects of training, particularly in the interpretation field. With the organization's help Trust staff have been able to gain expertise in both Europe and the United States, where the US National Parks Service offers much to learn from.

In a sense every new property acquired by the Trust and every new venture initiated has been an act of faith. This is as much the case now as it was in the early days when the gap between resources and responsibilities could only be closed by a boldness of vision and vigorous action that at times seemed rash. With more than a hundred properties in its care, ranging from mountains to mansions, from castles to cliffs, each new acquisition is in the nature of an experiment. The

Threave House and Garden.

Horticultural students at Threave Garden.

The staff of Robert Smail's Printing Works, about 1900, with Robert Cowan Smail (top right), son of the founder.

engagement with conservation cannot be separated from public response, for that response is the wider recognition of the need to safeguard Scotland's natural and historical environment upon which the Trust's work depends.

Scotland is a small country and the pressure of both tourism and development is increasing. The Trust's awareness of this, and of the importance of matching an accelerated pace of operation, is shaping its aims and policy for the future. Most threatened now are Scotland's countryside and coastline, and these are likely to claim particular attention from the Trust. The implementation of Trust policy will continue to be directed by the need for balance. The environmental future cannot be divorced from the economic present and the livelihood of an area's human inhabitants must be protected as well as the environment itself. There is a growing understanding of the interdependence of the two.

In a sense, too, each of the Trust's properties is a reflection of community, though not all as obviously so as the islands, or as towns such as Culross and Dunkeld. Each property is also a contribution to a community, helping to focus its historic and current significance. The most recent property to open to the public is a striking illustration of this. Robert Smail's Printing Works was operating in Innerleithen until 1986. At first sight there is nothing particularly remarkable about a small town printing works, but this one had continued working with equipment dating from the turn of the century in a trade that has experienced huge technological advances. In addition, there was a record of every print job carried out since the business had started 120 years before.

The printing business was started by Robert Smail in 1866. By that time Innerleithen had grown from a village to a sizeable town, largely as a result of the textile industry which expanded vigorously in Border towns in the early nineteenth century. Smail moved into printing from

The Composing Room, Robert Smail's Printing Works.

the boot and shoe business, buying the premises next door so that he could build over a mill-lade running from Leithen Water, which provided water power for his machinery.

Smail's works carried out a variety of work for the local community. He printed notices, posters, invitations, announcements, business cards, letterheads, serving the multifarious printing needs of a busy community and in particular of the textile industry. Between May 1893 and March 1916 Smail's printed a weekly newspaper, the *St Ronan's Standard and Effective Advertiser*. Most of the issues survive, and provide a chronicle of Innerleithen and its environs for that period. Its demise in 1916, in the middle of the First World War, was due to lack of staff. The paper itself records an appeal to the local conscription tribunal to exempt one of Smail's employees who had been called up: the appeal was lost.

Latterly the business was run by Cowan Smail, Robert's grandson, who retired in 1986. It was quite by chance that the Trust discovered that the printing works were closing down and likely to be dismantled; indeed some material was literally on the pavement awaiting disposal when it was rescued. It was realized at once that Smail's Printing Works was not just an out-of-date business with a certain curiosity value but an archive of the printing trade and of the Innerleithen community.

Over the decades very little had changed and very little had been thrown away. From the beginnning there seemed to be a resistance to new technology combined with astuteness in using the old. Smail's used water power when most presses were run by steam. In the 1880s Smail's moved to more modern methods with the acquisition of a lithographic press, but about half a century later the process was abandoned, in favour of continuing only with letterpress. This was at a time when letterpress printing was beginning to be superceded, although it has an unrivalled quality. In 1930 a Crossley engine was installed which used gas to power the presses. Later the machinery ran on electric power. The last press to be acquired was an 'Original Heidelberg' which came in 1953. Thereafter there was no major modernization.

In addition to the printing presses a treasure house of other material survives. In the composing room there is everything that the compositor needs, all very much as it was found when Cowan Smail retired. The type itself is stored in cases, and as well as the different fonts of lead type there is large wooden poster type. There are the formes in which the type was set; made-up formes of type for regular repeat jobs were kept. These in themselves tell us something about the community's needs. There are blocks with all kinds of regularly-used logos and illustrations. And there are the compositors' tools, setting sticks in which the pieces of type are first set, quoins which are used to wedge the type firmly in place, mallets and planers for making sure the type is level. The value of this survival is that it not only provides a record of a particular phase of the printing industry, it is still serviceable. Visitors are able to see a printworks in operation, and can try typesetting for themselves, a skill that required seven years of apprenticeship to master.

Other immensely valuable survivors are the guardbooks, in which a sample of every print job is preserved. A printer was obliged to keep samples of each job for six months; it is very rare to find records maintained for over a century. The guardbooks provide an archive of the work of a small town jobbing printer, but they also document the life of the town itself. The main business activities, community events and social occasions are reflected, and in turn provide a picture of life in and around Innerleithen. The printing works, with its High Street shop front, had a conspicuous role in the community, providing a service and in different ways chronicling its fortunes.

In preparing Smail's Printing Works for the visitor the Trust has had to carry out radical restoration work to the fabric of the building, which was very run down when it was taken over. A reproduction of the original mill wheel has been re-installed, and the system of pulleys and wheels that linked it with the machinery still exists, although water is no longer the source of power. The premises are preserved as a working environment, and although some changes have been required to make it safe care has been taken not to destroy the ambience of a printshop. The objects themselves, the sound of the presses, the printed products that come from them, the smell of printer's ink, all contribute to the experience, and make the Printing Works an intriguing example of living history. It is not a fossilized segment of the past, nor is it a reconstruction: it is a print works operating as it might have done at the beginning of this century, a modest but illuminating revitalization.

An injection of new life can take many forms. It is easy in the age of heritage awareness to assume that anything that belongs to the past is by definition worth preserving. This is clearly not so. But what has been a fundamental part of the Trust's policy is that everything that is worth preserving should be genuinely 'for the benefit of the nation', not only accessible to the public but maintained with a real understanding of what the inheritance means in the contexts of past, present and future. One way of doing this is by reviving a business, or a home, or a stretch of land, that made a distinctive contribution to its environs, or which has something particular to tell us about how we lived once and how we have come to where we are now. To achieve this requires the balance that has become the Trust's watchword, of resources, of interests, of needs, of responsibilities.

The Trust now has over 200,000 members, and these members are the foundations of the Trust's continuing. Sixty percent of the Trust's revenue comes from its members through membership subscriptions, legacies and investment income: a growing membership is an insurance for the future. Growth fosters activity, activity brings achievement which in turn encourages new members. Visitors to the properties in the care of the National Trust for Scotland have steadily increased in numbers over the six decades of its existence. In 1990 visitor figures reached the two million mark. These figures are an inarguable measure of success, a public demonstration of the Trust's continuing achievement, but they are also a challenge. Visitors mean wear and tear. The welcoming of visitors means a responsibility to educate, not only about the land and the life it has sustained, but about how the land and its life can be fostered and protected.

Behind this responsibility lie the commitment and sheer hard work that is required to look after both the properties and their visitors. The work of conservation and interpretation is continuous. The process of maintenance, restoration, redecoration, arranging special exhibitions and events, running education programmes and courses, has many facets. This work is supported by many organizations, individuals and groups of volunteers, and is carried out in co-operation with a number of bodies. The broad spectrum of involvement is itself a reflection of the centrality of the Trust's concerns. There is now a greater awareness than ever before of the fact that our future depends on a sensitive and sensible attitude to the present and the past. The National Trust for Scotland has known this for sixty years, and continues to demonstrate the courage of its convictions.

The Summer House at Brodick Castle.

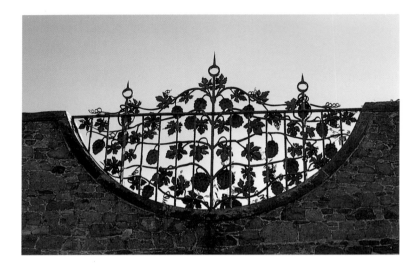

Wrought iron gates at Priorwood Garden,
Melrose, made in the Kippen Smiddy.

Index

INDEX

INDEX

Please help support the work of the National Trust for Scotland by becoming a member. Membership gives you free entry into over 200 properties in Scotland and over 300 properties of the National Trust in England, Wales and Northern Ireland. Send for a membership leaflet and details about the properties to: The National Trust for Scotland, 5 Charlotte Square, Edinburgh EH2 4DU.
For readers in the United States of America, please write to:
Scottish Heritage U.S.A., Inc.
P.O. Box 457
Pinehurst, N.C. 28374.

Lewis

A836 Thurso

A895

🌂 35. **Fair Isle** (Midway between Orkney and Shetland)

Harris

Ullapool

Properties in the care of the
🌂 National Trust for Scotland

🌂 73. **St Kilda** (60 miles west of Harris)

🌂 55. **Inverewe Garden**
🌂 24. **Corrieshalloch Gorge**

Skye

52. **Hugh Millers' Cottage**

🌂 81. **Torridon** A832
74. **Shieldaig Island**

11. **Boath Doocot**
🌂 15. **Brodie Castle**
Nairn
🌂 28. **Culloden**
87. **Clava Cairns**

Fraserburgh

A92

A96

38. **Fyvie Castle**
🌂 45. **Haddo House**

🌂 78. **Strome Castle**
🌂 4. **Balmacara Estate**
🌂 37. **Falls of Glomach**
1. **Abertarff House**
Inverness
60. **Leith Hall**
🌂 66. **Pitmedden Garden**
A920
70. **Provost Ross's House** (Aberdeen Maritime Museum)

🌂 58. **Kintail and Morvich**
22. **Castle Fraser**
Inverurie
25. **Craigievar Castle**
A980
A944
Aberdeen

20. **Canna**
27. **Crathes Castle, Garden and Estate**
33. **Drum Castle**

A830
🌂 42. **Glenfinnan Monument**

A86

A93

Fort William

Tobermory

🌂 41. **Glencoe and Dalness**
61. **Linn of Tummel**
🌂 64. **Pass of Killiecrankie**
🌂 51. **House of Dun**
🌂 26. **Craigower**
🌂 7. **Barrie's Birthplace**
Pitlochry
Forfar
🌂 2. **Angus Folk Museum**

8. **Ben Lawers**
A827
🌂 34. **Dunkeld**
47. **The Hermitage**

77. **Staffa**
🌂 95. **Macquarie Mausoleum**
18. **Burg**
56. **Iona**
A849
Oban
Crianlarich
A85
12. **Branklyn Garden**
Perth
🌂 5. **Balmerino Abbey**
Dundee

Mull

98. **Menstrie Castle**
96. **Kippen Smiddy**
36. **Falkland Palace**
🌂 49. **Hill of Tarvit**
A93
🌂 93. **Scotstarvit Tower**

9. **Ben Lomond**
🌂 32. **Dollar Glen**
🌂 86. **Castle Campbell**
🌂 57. **Kellie Castle and Garden**

31. **Cunninghame Graham Memorial**
101. **Sailor's Walk**
Stirling
17. **Bucinch and Ceardach**
6. **Bannockburn**
🌂 29. **Culross** (Study and Town House)
🌂 89. **Culross: the Palace**
🌂 90. **Dirleton Castle**

48. **The Hill House**
97. **Stirling Castle Visitor Centre**
65. **The Pineapple**
🌂 67. **Preston Mill / Phantassie Doocot**
23. **Castlehill**
85. **Antonine Wall**
100. **Plewland's House**
🌂 46. **Hamilton House**
92. **Preston Tower**

63. **Parklea Farm**
99. **Linlithgow Houses**
50. **House of the Binns**
🌂 54. **Inveresk Lodge Garden**
🌂 72. **St Abb's Head**
53. **Hutchesons' Hall**
🌂 69. **Provan Hall**
🌂 59. **Caiy Stone**
🌂 59. **Lamb's House**

84. **Weaver's Cottage**
🌂 79. **Tenement House**
Glasgow
39. **Georgian House and Charlotte Square**
Berwick-upon-Tweed

43. **Greenbank Garden**
88. **Crookston Castle**
62. **Malleny Garden**
40. **Gladstone's Land**

Gigha
🌂 14. **Goatfell**
10. **Blackhill**
75. **Robert Smail's Printing Works**
🌂 82. **Turret House**

Ardrossan
68. **Priorwood Garden**
A708

13. **Brodick Castle, and Country Park**

Campbeltown
🌂 3. **Bachelors' Club**
Ayr

🌂 30. **Culzean Castle and Country Park**
🌂 44. **Grey Mare's Tail**
🌂 76. **Souter Johnnie's Cottage**

NTS Regions
Central & Tayside
Grampian
Highland
Lothian, Fife & Borders
West (includes Strathclyde and Dumfries & Galloway)

Dumfries
🌂 16. **Bruce's Stone**
🌂 21. **Carlyle's Birthplace**

Stranraer
Castle Douglas
🌂 80. **Threave Garden**
🌂 94. **Threave Castle**
83. **Venniehill**
🌂 71. **Rockcliffe**
91. **Glenluce Abbey Glebe**

miles
0 10 20 30 40 50
0 10 20 30 40 50 60 70 80
kilometres